A New Vision for Housing

Chris Holmes

Routledge
Taylor & Francis Group

LONDON AND NEW YORK

First published 2006
by Routledge
2 Park Square, Milton Park, Abingdon, Oxon OX14 4RN

Simultaneously published in the USA and Canada
by Routledge
270 Madison Avenue, New York, NY 10016

Routledge is an imprint of the Taylor & Francis Group

Typeset in Sabon and Gill Sans by
Florence Production Ltd, Stoodleigh, Devon
Printed and bound in Great Britain by
TJ International Ltd, Padstow, Cornwall

British Library Cataloguing in Publication Data
A catalogue record for this book is available from the British Library

Library of Congress Cataloging in Publication Data
Holmes, Chris.
    A new vision for housing / Christopher Holmes. – 1st ed.
      p. cm.
    Includes bibliographical references and index.
      1. Housing – Great Britain.   2. Housing policy – Great Britain.
    3. Public housing – Great Britain.   I. Title.
    HD7333.A3H656 2005
    353.5'85'0941 – dc22   2005008345

ISBN10: 0–415–36080–3 (hbk)
ISBN10: 0–415–36081–1 (pbk)

ISBN13: 9–78–0–415–36080–7 (hbk)
ISBN13: 9–78–0–415–36081–4 (pbk)

Contents

Illustrations

Plates

Graphs

Tables

Preface

Building sustainable communities is now a central theme of the Government's housing policy, linked to wider objectives such as reducing social exclusion. Achieving this aim may be helped by understanding better what has caused social polarisation, and what lessons from history can inform future policies.

Today, while most homeowners live in homes with gardens, in suburban or rural areas, benefiting from rising capital assets, many tenants live in neighbourhoods of concentrated poverty. Increasing numbers of young people cannot afford to buy and record numbers of homeless families are trapped in temporary accommodation.

This book traces the different policy mistakes that have given rise to this inequality, and puts forward new proposals:

- creating mixed income communities across all housing areas;
- ending the use of temporary accommodation for homeless families;
- building 300,000 homes a year, with at least 90,000 for people who cannot afford to buy;
- reducing the divide in housing wealth.

I would like to thank the many people who have contributed to the research and writing of this book. The work was done as a Visiting Research Fellow with the Institute for Public Policy

Research, with funding for the project donated by Chris Ingram, the Focus Housing Group, the Notting Hill Housing Group and Riverside Housing Association. I would like to thank Rachel O'Brien and Sue Regan for their many helpful contributions from the initial ideas about the project to the production of the final text.

I am grateful to many people with whom I have discussed the ideas developed in the book. I would like to thank: Karen Buck MP for her powerful descriptions of the severe overcrowding experienced by constituents coming to her surgery quoted in Chapter 11; all those whom I met on my visits to Liverpool for Chapter 10, especially Richard Kemp, Ken Perry, Matthew Gardiner and Deborah Shackleton; every one I met for the projects described in Chapter 12 on Oases of Excellence, and in particular: Richard Best and Julie Cowans from the Joseph Rowntree Foundation; Ken Perry from the Plus Housing Group in Liverpool; Iain Tuckett from Coin Street Community Builders; and Andrew Watson from Walterton and Elgin Community Homes. I would also like to thank Peter Williams and Steve Wilcox for their comments on Chapter 13 on Sharing Housing Wealth, and to Steve also for access to his unparalleled knowledge of revealing statistics.

While the research and writing of the book were carried out as a Visiting Research Fellow of IPPR, all of the opinions expressed in the book are my own.

Finally I would like to thank Hattie Llewelyn-Davies for her support through every stage, from her initial encouragement to embark on writing a book and her invariably perceptive and valuable comments on all the chapters.

Chapter 1

Homes fit for heroes

A Victorian failure

For all its grand achievements the Victorian era left a scandalous legacy of slum housing. A road to reform was pioneered by a small number of philanthropists and enlightened employers, but against the scale of the problem the action was pitiful.

During the nineteenth century, England changed from being a largely rural society to a predominantly urban one. Millions of people flocked to the cities when the new factories were being built and many lived in overcrowded tenements with no proper sanitation.

A succession of enquiries documented the nature and extent of housing and public health problems.[1] Edwin Chadwick, the Secretary of the Poor Law Commissioners, wrote the first major report, the *Report on the Condition of the Labouring Poor*, in 1842. Prompted by a violent outbreak of fever in Spitalfields in the East End of London, the report demonstrated the link between poverty, bad housing and disease.

The central belief of the sanitary reformers was that they could improve the living conditions of the poor by reducing epidemic disease and that by restoring health they could raise earning power sufficiently to allow the renting of decent houses. Yet when cholera and typhus had been quelled by sanitation measures in all the cities, the housing situation was seen to have grown, if anything, worse.

The average number of people living in each house increased throughout the century, despite the efforts of the reformers.

The number of people living in England and Wales grew from 1.6 million in 1801 to 4.3 million in 1871. However, over the same period the excess of families over the number of houses available had more than doubled, from 321,000 in 1801 to 790,000 in 1871.[2]

Between the 1850s and 1870s the demolition of homes to make way for the railways, the influx of new workers and rising rents made overcrowding still worse than ever. In the 1880s there were outbreaks of popular unrest, notably in London, Birmingham and Manchester, which shocked political leaders and middle class opinion, who feared the kind of revolutionary uprising which had taken place elsewhere in Europe. The Royal Commission on the Housing of the Working Class was set up in 1885 as a response to this discontent. It took extensive evidence from different areas of the country, especially on conditions of overcrowding and rent levels:

> It was common practice in London for each family to have only a single room for the rent, of which nearly half of them paid between 25 per cent and 50 per cent of their wages. A contributory cause was the existence of the disreputable middle man.[3]

In his powerful descriptions of poverty in London, Andrew Mearns, a leading Congregational Minister, captured the dreadful conditions endured by the poorest families.

> Every room in these rotten and reeking tenements houses a family, often two. In one cellar a sanitary inspector reports finding a father, mother, three children and four pigs! In another room seven people are living in one underground kitchen, and a little dead child lying in the same room. Another apartment contains father, mother and six children, two of whom are ill with scarlet fever. In another nine brothers and sisters, from 29 years of age downwards, live, eat and sleep together.[4]

Octavia Hill is best known for her distinctive approach to housing management. With financial help from rich supporters, notably John Ruskin, she bought up houses and courts in the worst areas she could find, and sought to encourage tenants to take pride in their homes. As her reputation grew she took on and trained more female housing managers (always women!) who worked under her supervision. She did not compromise with tenants who did not meet her standards. She accepted for re-housing those who showed signs of wishing to improve their condition and took no further interest in those who did not.

> As soon as I entered into possession, each family who would not pay, or who led clearly immoral lives, were ejected. The rooms they vacated were cleansed, the tenants who showed signs of improvement moved into them.[5]

In her groundbreaking study of the management of council housing Anne Power sums up Octavia Hill's beliefs and legacy:

> Octavia Hill cannot be readily classified as either a social reformer or as a successful businesswoman. Her main contribution was to develop a management technique, which brought slum property up to minimal standards for the day at a cost that the mass of slum dwellers could afford. She spoke out against displacement of poor people, against impersonal blocks, and against political control of landlord services. She advocated meticulous management, continuous repairs, tenants' priorities for improvements, resident jobs, women's employment, and tenants' control over their own lives. But she did not understand that with over one million sharing households the relatively small scale of efforts would be overtaken and to a large extent devalued.[6]

Over the second half of the century a handful of reformers, philanthropists and enlightened employers embarked on a range of initiatives to provide decent homes for working class tenants.

Lord Shaftesbury's Society for Improving the Condition of the Labouring Classes was set up in the 1840s, the first not-for-profit body seeking to provide new homes for working class tenants. The Four Per Cent Society was set up in 1852 by a group of Jewish philanthropists to relieve overcrowding in the East End of London, becoming the first housing trust to cater specifically for an ethnic minority.

The Peabody Trust was founded in 1862 with a generous donation from an American, George Peabody, who had made his fortune as a prosperous merchant in England. Dedicated to helping 'the poor of London' the Peabody Trust built blocks of tenement flats and by 1867 had provided over 5,000 dwellings.[7] Several others, including Sydney Waterlow's Improved Dwellings Company, the Guinness Trust and the Samuel Lewis Trust, followed its example. The densely built tenement flats built by these trusts later became the model for the London County Council's walk-up blocks (typically four storey blocks of flats, with no lifts, and front doors opening off the balconies on each floor).

These associations funded their housing schemes by taking out loans and paying a dividend to investors of between 4 per cent and 5 per cent. They aimed to demonstrate that it was financially viable to provide self-contained flats for working class families. However, it was only the better paid artisans who were able to afford the rents. Even the homes of the charitable trusts were beyond the reach of the poorer labourers.

Gareth Stedman Jones has pointed out that the tenancy rules of Peabody excluded the poorest:

> Despite the predominantly seasonal character of employment in London, rents had to be paid in advance and no arrears were allowed. Applications were not considered without a reference from an employer, although in the case of a casual labourer this was almost by definition impossible. A substantial number of the very poor were widows or deserted wives, or poor mothers of large families, who earned a small living as washerwomen, but Peabody rules dictated that washing could only be done in the laundry, and that it could only be the tenant's own clothing.
>
> All but the most prosperous of the working class living in the central area (of London) lived with their families in

one room units. But Peabody rules did not permit more than one person to inhabit one room ... The economic effect of these regulations was to put Peabody Dwellings out of reach of the casual poor.[8]

Most of the new Housing and Public Health Acts that were passed focused on sanitary provisions to prevent disease caused by severe overcrowding, polluted water and dangerous sewerage. The worst 'rookeries' – the dense, urban slums – were cleared, but not replaced by new homes that the displaced residents could afford.

The number of new homes built for working class families was tiny in relation to the scale of housing need. Throughout the nineteenth century the dominant view was the rejection of state action in providing homes for working class tenants. Despite all the evidence of market failure, politicians and most reformers clung stubbornly to their reliance on private landlords and voluntary initiative.

One of the clearest statements of the prevailing ideology was a speech by the Earl of Derby, a leading member of the Conservative Party, made in Liverpool in 1871. After stressing the need for urgent action 'to provide every man, woman and child with a clean, wholesome and decent lodging', he went on:

It is vitally essential that this work we now have in hand should be done by private enterprise. Either it will pay or it will not. If it will not – but that is a hypothesis I do not accept for an instant – it is no light matter to require the local governing body of the town to provide homes for the poor at less than their cost price. For if a poor man, not being a pauper, has a right to be supplied with a home at less than it costs, why not the food also – the one is as necessary as the other – and then you come to nothing less than a system of universal outdoor relief.[9]

A small number of employers, notably several prominent Quakers, built settlements to house their workers. Port Sunlight, south of Birkenhead, was funded by W. H. Lever, as a demonstration of his vision of a profit-sharing company. Titus Salt built a model village next to his new factory at Shipley in West Yorkshire, with 800 cottages in long terraces but with a variety of styles and for different sizes of families, based on a survey of his employees' needs. The Bournville village in Birmingham was not devised solely as a 'company town', but as a model village for residents from a range of backgrounds. Joseph Rowntree's model village was built at New Earswick outside York (see Chapter 12).

The garden city movement, founded by Ebenezer Howard, developed the most ambitious new settlements. His vision was to create self-contained communities, with houses, factories and social facilities, to enable people to escape from the overcrowded urban slums. The first was built at Letchworth Garden City in Hertfordshire, followed by the development at Welwyn Garden City. However, the absence of public subsidy meant that only middle class families were able to afford the prices of the new homes.

Hampstead Garden Suburb was a different form of planned new settlement, conceived by Henrietta Barnett in 1903. She was a well-known social reformer, a friend of Octavia Hill's and married to Canon Barnett, the Warden of Toynbee Hall, the pioneering East End settlement.

Her vision was to build an integrated community for all social classes on the fringe of London. The cheaper cottages were built close to the newly opened tube at Golders Green, but, unfortunately, rising rents put the new homes beyond the reach of working class families. It soon became a highly desirable suburb, occupied only by affluent middle class residents.

The architect for Hampstead Garden Suburb was Raymond Unwin, who had also designed Letchworth and Welwyn with his partner Barry Parker. He was a committed socialist, whose thinking had been strongly influenced by the ideas of John Ruskin and William Morris. Most of Unwin and Parker's early architectural work involved designing rural houses for middle class families but they went on to design several of the first local authority housing estates.

The new developments were in striking contrast to the densely built city streets. In 1912 Unwin wrote a pamphlet *Nothing Gained by Overcrowding*, which argued that no new housing should be built at more than 12 houses per acre.[10] Almost all the model settlements built by the employers and the garden city movement were houses with gardens.

It was not until 1890 that local authorities were given statutory powers to build new housing, but even then there was no duty on councils to do so.

The London County Council (LCC), Glasgow and Liverpool were the first councils to build directly. The first LCC homes were suburban estates on the edge of London's built up area, starting with the Totterdown Fields Estate at Tooting, at the terminus of an LCC tramway, followed by White Hart Lane in Tottenham. One of the most successful was at Old Oak Lane estate in Hammersmith, where 'the houses were built in a variety of groups and around small open spaces, which avoided both the monotony of the bye-law street and the somewhat artificial rusticity of the garden suburb'.[11]

By the early years of the twentieth century the pressure for greater state action was increasing. The newly created Labour Party was growing in strength and housing for working class people was one its priorities. In 1906 the Liberal Party was elected to power with an ambitious agenda for social reform.

However, what really transformed the political mood was the First World War, which shattered the complacency of Britain's ruling elite. By the end of the war, tackling the housing problem had become the top priority for domestic policy. 'To let them (our heroes) come home from horrible, water logged trenches to something little better than a pigsty would indeed be criminal' was the warning given by the local government minister that vividly expressed the popular mood.[12] A new promise was voiced by the Prime Minister, David Lloyd George, in his famous promise of 'homes fit for heroes'.

The importance at last being given to the housing programme was not only due to social concern. At the end of the war there was a widespread fear of a popular uprising, following the Bolshevik revolution in Russia in 1917 and awareness of the strength of the revolutionary movement in Germany. The promise of decent homes for the returning soldiers and their families was seen by leading politicians as one of the most important ways to quell social unrest.

Fortunately, a great deal of work had been done during the war years to prepare the ground for a large-scale housing programme. In particular, two reports had a major influence on the development of the future policies.

In 1916 the Government had set up a Reconstruction Committee, with the brief to prepare ambitious plans for post-war legislation and policies, and which set up specialist groups to study key issues. One of these was a Housing Panel, which produced a detailed report on future housing requirements. Progressives, including the leading Fabian Beatrice Webb, dominated its membership. The key section on the need to build 300,000 homes in the first year after the war was written by one of the specially appointed experts, Seebohm Rowntree.[13]

Central to the Panel's proposals was the belief that the Government should intervene directly in the post-war provision of working class housing. In the view of an influential social historian 'the Panel's statement marked the first important public document in the development of modern housing policy'.[14]

Another key report came from the Tudor Walters Committee on the standards of post-war local authority housing. Building on earlier experience of the model settlements and the garden city movement, the report developed these into detailed and comprehensive recommendations for new housing.

Many of the proposals were the work of Raymond Unwin, who had left his architectural practice in 1916 to take up a senior post in the Ministry of Munitions. In his new role he had masterminded a number of large housing schemes including a development of 1,000 homes at Well Hall, Eltham for employees at the Royal Arsenal in Woolwich which was hailed by one international expert 'as a community which from the architectural standpoint is without equal in the world'.[15]

The Tudor Walters Committee recommended that new housing should be built at densities of not more than 12 to an acre, that higher space standards should be implemented – 855 square feet for a three bedroom non-parlour house and 1,055 square feet for the parlour type, with a separate sitting room and upstairs bathroom and WC – and that there should also be a greater emphasis on the environment outside the home.

The proposals on design for new housing were strongly influenced by the ideas of the garden city movement, but rejected what critics saw as the over-elaborate, romanticised features of the homes built at Letchworth and elsewhere, such as the emphasis on gable ends and bay windows. The new emphasis was on greater simplicity of style, with carefully placed and proportioned doors and windows:

> The report was to give a particular stamp to the character of local authority housing, almost all in new low-density estates, which at the time was accepted as the best and natural way of housing the urban working classes.[16]

The landmark achievement was the 1919 Housing Act, known as the Addison Act, named after the Minister, Christopher Addison, a Radical Liberal – and later Labour MP. It was strongly backed by a housing lobby outside Parliament, led by representatives of local authorities and professional experts. The importance of this Act was expressed by a historian of this period:

> The great changes effected by the Housing Act of 1919 are almost too simply and easily put, and of these the greatest is so simple as almost to seem unimportant: housing of the working classes became a duty of the state. The statute envisioned housing activity by government, a clear break with the prewar past. Then, private enterprise had been responsible for 90 per cent of such building. Now a partnership of the central government and the local authorities would be in the business of housing.
>
> The premise of governmental responsibility and action had been common ground to all wartime reform groups. It was adopted here, once and for all – a principle that, as it proved, was the greatest and most enduring consequence of the Act.[17]

Providence Place, Stepney, 1909
London Metropolitan Archives

Carefully detailed semis at Hale, Cheshire, 1922
BBC Hulton Picture Library

Chestnut Avenue in 1910, New Earswick
Rowntree Housing Trust

Cleaning the Morris Eight
BBC Hulton Picture Library

The euphoria that greeted the successful passing of the Act was short-lived. The fear of a revolutionary uprising had faded. After some fierce battles in Cabinet the views of the Ministers who put repaying war debts over social welfare prevailed, and the housing programme was cut. Addison's arguments were blocked by Austen Chamberlain, the Chancellor of the Exchequer, and Addison resigned from the Cabinet.

The housing programme was revived in 1924, following the election of the first Labour Government. The new Minister was a Scottish MP, John Wheatley, who had been Chair of Housing in Glasgow and was known to have a strong commitment to public housing. He successfully restored political support for an ambitious housing programme, although with lower subsidies than under the Addison Act.

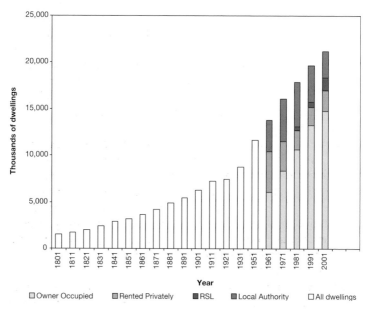

Graph 1.1 Growth in number of dwellings (1801–2001)

Note: Numbers for each tenure are shown from 1961

Due to a shortage of workers in the building trade, only 73,000 houses were completed in 1923. By 1926, however, an extra 160,000 building workers were employed and the number of new homes rose to 273,000. So the housing programme also reduced unemployment through the creation of new jobs.

The homes built under the Addison and Wheatley Housing Acts were immensely popular with the tenants who lived in them. They were undoubtedly superior to the homes being built for working class tenants by private enterprise. The rents were too high for the poorest families, despite the government subsidies, but the new homes enabled many thousands of working class families to escape from overcrowded slums.

In 1930 the priorities of the housing programme changed. The Greenwood Act, named after the Labour Minister of Health Arthur Greenwood, laid the foundations for future slum clearance programmes. Its critical provision was that local authorities were given subsidies for the number of people displaced and re-housed. This was aimed to prevent the pre-war practices of clearing the slums and simply evicting the former tenants. It also made it easier for local authorities to house the larger, poor families who suffered the worst housing conditions. However, under the Coalition Government formed in 1931 the quality of new homes was reduced, with more blocks of flats and fewer houses with gardens.

Despite the local authority house building programme three quarters of the new homes built between the wars – more than three million – were for private ownership. Under the Chamberlain Housing Act of 1922 new private homes were eligible for government subsidies and a combination of falling house building costs and low interest rates made house purchase exceptionally attractive. The result was a huge growth of middle class suburbs, especially in outer London.

The semi-detached homes in the suburbs and the council estates were both strongly influenced by the architectural ideas of the garden city tradition and recommendations of the Tudor Walters report. Although the report was primarily directed at local authorities and had the status of an official manual, its detailed and practical advice on house layouts was widely used by speculative builders.

Yet the philosophies and values that shaped the two types of housing led to widening differences. The council estates were planned to encourage a strong sense of community, reflected in building more terraces rather than semi-detached houses and the provision of public open space and community centres. In contrast, the design of the suburban semis stressed values of individuality, expressed in the bay windows, porches, cul-de-sacs, and private back and front gardens.

Many of the new suburban homeowners had escaped from the inner city to achieve a higher social status and sought to express this in a variety of different ways, such as the house name, the assiduously tended gardens and the careful furnishing of the front room.

The tensions between the homeowner and the council tenant were exposed most dramatically in the extraordinary saga of the Cutteslowe wall in north Oxford in 1934. The residents of a newly completed private development, bizarrely named 'the Urban Housing Estate', complained to the builders about nuisance allegedly being caused by tenants on the adjoining council estate, claiming this would lower the value of their homes.

In response the builder erected a seven-foot-high wall, topped by iron spikes, which prevented the council tenants from walking through the estate to the main road which led to the centre of the city. Despite vigorous protests, huge media publicity, heated debates in the council chamber and legal action in the courts, it was almost twenty-five years before the wall was finally taken down, allowing tenants on the council estate to walk down the road on the private housing estate to gain access to the main road. Until then they faced a detour of almost half a mile to the nearest shops, the local secondary school or the buses into the city centre.[18]

In the twenty years from 1919 to 1939 a total of four million new homes were built. Just over a million were built by local authorities and almost three million by private enterprise, of which over 400,000 were subsidised. The highest annual programmes were achieved in the 1930s, with over 300,000 homes a year being built, many contributing to a massive growth of suburban home ownership.

By the outbreak of the Second World War the future shape of English housing was set. Home ownership was growing, as many middle class and better-off working class families opted increasingly to move to semi-detached homes in the suburbs. Council housing was becoming established as the best hope for most working class families, although it remained accessible to relatively few of the poorest.

A pattern of social and physical segregation was becoming clear. There had always been a hierarchy of housing provision in villages, towns and cities, but most communities contained people from a range of incomes and classes. Only owner-occupiers now occupied many of the newly expanding suburbs, while most council housing was being built in the urban areas.

The Second World War

The second critical moment when a different housing future seemed possible was at the end of the Second World War, as it had at the end of the First. As the people of Britain prepared to vote at the General Election in 1945 an opinion poll found that four people out of ten put housing as the most important problem for the next Government.

Let's Face the Future, the election manifesto on which the Labour Party won its landslide victory, was clear in its promise: 'Housing will be one of the greatest and earliest tests of our Government's real determination to put the nation first. We will proceed with a housing programme at maximum possible speed until every working family in this island has a good standard of accommodation.'[19]

The task the new Government faced was daunting. During the war almost half a million homes had been destroyed by bombing, and another half a million were very severely damaged. More than half of all households rented from private landlords, where many properties were run-down and poorly

Cutteslowe wall, Summertown, 1934
Oxford Mail

Cutteslowe wall finally being taken down, 1938
Oxford Mail

equipped. The worst squalor and overcrowding was experienced
in the densely populated neighbourhoods of the great cities.

No new houses had been built for six years. The number of
people working in the construction industry had fallen to a third
of its pre-war level. After years of being separated by the war,
millions of families wanted a new home where they could settle
and bring up their children.

Responsibility for the housing programme was with the
Minister of Health, Nye Bevan. Despite the huge pressure to
build as many homes as possible, he insisted on keeping to the
improved standards recommended by the Dudley Committee in
1943, especially raising the size of a new three-bedroom home
from 750 to 900 square feet. The response to his critics was
that 'we shall be judged in twenty years time not by the *number*
of homes that we have built but by the *quality* of homes'.[20]

Introducing the new Housing Bill in 1949, Bevan argued that:

> It is entirely undesirable that on modern housing estates
> only one type of citizen should live. If we are to enable citi-
> zens to lead a full life, if they are each to be aware of the
> problems of their neighbours, then they should all be drawn
> from different sections of the community. We should try to
> introduce what was always the lovely feature of English and
> Welsh villages, where the doctor, the grocer, the butcher
> and the farm labourer all lived in the same street.[21]

As a symbol of that aim, he said, the Bill would sweep away
all reference to 'the housing of the working classes'.

The most notable innovation in Labour's post-war policy was
the new towns programme. The original inspiration was the
vision for garden cities first set out by Ebenezer Howard. For
half a century the garden city movement had campaigned for
the development of planned new settlements, outside the overcrowded cities, that would provide new homes, jobs and
community amenities. Two government commissioned reports
were important influences on the new policies.

The Barlow Commission had been set up by Neville
Chamberlain in 1937 in response to growing concern at the

uncontrolled expansion of London and the depressed areas of the north of England. After three years of exhaustive study, the Commission recommended controls over the location of industry in and around London, limits on the growth of conurbations and the building of garden cities. Abercrombie's Greater London Plan in 1944 set out a visionary framework for the future, with the creation of a circular green belt around London, a massive overspill programme and the development of eight new towns for 400,000 people.[22]

Labour's election manifesto in 1945 did not include any proposals for new towns, but within weeks of his appointment the new Minister for Planning, Lewis Silkin, circulated proposals for legislation to create new towns and shortly afterwards Lord Reith was asked to chair a committee to draw up detailed plans. There were two key principles in the proposals of the Reith Committee: that the new towns should be 'self-contained and balanced communities for working and living'.[23] They were to be *self-contained* in providing for the need of everyday living, including work, shops and other services, and *balanced* in providing for people from a mix of different social and economic groups.

The first new town, Stevenage, was announced in November 1946. By the end of 1949 seven more new towns followed on the fringes of London, two towns in the north-east, two in Scotland and one in Wales. In total the new towns were planned to provide homes for 559,000 people.

By 1951 a million new homes had been built in England four-fifths of them by local authorities. The number of permanent new homes built each year rose from 139,000 in 1947 to 227,000 in 1948. Following the spending cuts made after the sterling crisis and devaluation, the number then fell to under 200,000 a year in 1949 and 1950.

Overall, however, the housing programme fell significantly short of what had been promised. From as early as 1946 the Government was criticised for delays in the housing programme and it was one of the Conservative Party's most consistent criticisms of Labour's record in office. Most historians of the record of the Labour Government agree that housing cannot be seen as one of its successes, despite some bold and innovative policies. So the question that must be asked is: why were the ambitious plans of 1945 not achieved?

The grave shortage of materials and labour in a war-ravaged country is clearly part of the explanation. Britain was forced to rely on imports for many building materials and foreign exchange to pay for them was very scarce. The building industry had shrunk dramatically during the war years, as construction workers had gone into the armed forces or to other vital war-related activity. It took time for the demobilisation of all the troops, especially those serving in the Far East, and for building firms to build up fully trained workforces.

The ill preparedness of many local authorities, which had the responsibility for building almost all the new homes, was another important factor. Some large councils, especially the LCC, had experience of carrying out large house building programmes, but many did not. In total there were over 1,700 councils with responsibility for housing, many of them small rural or urban district councils. Not all shared the belief in the need for many new council homes. Many lacked the managers, professional staff or administrative organisation required to plan and implement the programme the Government sought to achieve.

Some critics argued that local authorities were not capable of the key role they had been assigned and called for the setting up of a new national housing corporation. The Conservatives attacked the restrictions put on private builders, especially by a tough licensing system, which regulated the supply of building materials and labour.

In the debates over the Labour Government's housing record, one significant decision has been almost entirely ignored. The Labour Party manifesto said that a new Ministry of Planning and Local Government would be formed, which would be responsible for housing. Attlee ignored this commitment and kept housing within the Ministry of Health, as it had been since 1919. The important new factor, of course, was that in 1945 the Labour Government was committed to the huge task of creating a National Health Service – as well as the most ambitious programme of public house building ever undertaken.

Attlee entrusted both these tasks to Nye Bevan. He was an inspiring orator, the acknowledged leader of the left and a politician of vision. But in 1945 he had no experience as a minister. He was the only member of the Cabinet who had not served in the wartime coalition government. His most celebrated achievement was the creation of the National Health Service. In Peter Hennessy's words:

> 5 July 1948 was the second of Britain's finest hours in the brave and high-minded 1940s. That should not be forgotten ... when the trials and tribulations and the often fractious politics are given their due place in the post-war history of the United Kingdom. The NHS was and remains one of the finest institutions ever built by anyone anywhere.[24]

Bevan was undoubtedly exaggerating when he said, unwisely, that he 'gave only five minutes to housing a week'. Yet there is no doubt that most time and effort was given to health. It was inevitable that the housing programme would suffer. Bevan was right in resisting the pressure to cut standards in order to boost numbers, but that need not have been the choice.

No explanation is recorded in either Attlee's own memoirs or any history of the Labour Government of why the Prime Minister decided in 1945 to ignore the manifesto commitment to give responsibility for housing to a new ministry. Kenneth Morgan, the widely respected historian of the period and author of *Labour in Power* describes Attlee's decision as 'one of his most serious administrative mistakes'.[25] Attlee did eventually separate responsibility for health and housing, but not until 1950 when Hugh Dalton became Minister for Planning and Local Government.

The Labour Government did not have a comprehensive strategy for tackling the full range of housing problems facing the country. It had a target for tackling the shortage of housing by building new homes, but there were no clear policies for tackling the huge problems of housing obsolescence.

The tradition and approach of local authorities was fundamentally paternalistic. Their primary virtues were probity and commitment to public service. Being elected, councillors tended to believe that they knew what was best for people, and little priority was given to consulting tenants and those affected by future plans. Still less was given to encouraging active participation. These proved to be profound weaknesses as the role required from local authorities became hugely more complex in the years ahead.

What the Labour Government had not adequately recognised was the strength of aspirations for home ownership. It had been expressed in the huge suburban expansion in the 1930s. In the immediate post-war years it was blocked by the priority the Government gave to council building. New homes could not be built without a licence, and local authorities were building 80 per cent of new housing.

The experience of the post-war Government has important lessons for today. First, there was popular support for Labour's ambitious house building programme, but the promises were not matched by delivery. In particular, many local authorities lacked the skills and capacity that were needed. Second, the housing programme was not given the priority in ministerial time that was needed, and which Macmillan was to give – as instructed by Churchill – in the Conservative Government that followed.

Bevan was right in raising the standards of council housing and insisting on the importance of quality. Former council tenants still testify today to their popularity. 'I was brought up in a Bevan house and have believed in council housing ever since' is the personal credo of one well-known housing expert.[26] However, the failure to achieve the target for increasing the number of homes made it easier for the Conservatives to argue that a choice must be made between standards and numbers and to opt for cutting space standards and then quality. It was a fateful choice from which millions of council tenants were to suffer the consequences in the years to come.

Chapter 2

The rise of home ownership

It was the Conservative Party, not Labour as in 1945, which made housing a major issue in the 1951 General Election. At the Conservative conference the previous year the platform had been faced by a strongly backed resolution, inspired by the newly formed 'One Nation' group: to promise to build 300,000 new homes a year. The leadership reluctantly agreed.

The Conservative manifesto included this pledge. Almost every Conservative candidate featured housing as a critical issue in the election. By contrast the Labour Party was on the defensive as a result of its failure to meet the targets for building new homes. There was no reference to housing in the list of what the Labour Government had achieved since 1945.

The Minister for the newly created Cabinet post of Minister for Housing and Local Government was Harold Macmillan, charged by Churchill with the task of achieving the target that had been promised. In his diaries, *Tides of Fortune* (1945–1960), Macmillan describes his three years as Housing Minister not only as the most enjoyable of his Ministerial career but also as a crucial step in strengthening his reputation as an effective Minister.[1]

He tackled the house building challenge as if it were a military operation. He set up a new planning machinery within the Department, secured the support of the major building contractors, created regional boards – with representatives from employers and trade unions as well as local authorities and civil servants – and put enormous energy into touring the country to sustain the impetus of the programme. The target of 300,000 houses was successfully achieved in 1953.

By the mid 1950s Bevan's housing vision was being superseded by a very different ideological vision, that of a 'property owning democracy'. This was strongly promoted by Conservative politicians as a symbol of successful self-help, contrasted with the dependency of being a municipal tenant. The Government cut back plans for council house building and increased the share of the housing programme of building for sale – to 50 per cent. The primary responsibility both for building new homes and improving older homes was to be with the private sector.

The role of local authorities in future was in the main to be limited to clearing the slums. Subsidies were cut for other public sector house building, except for the new and expanding towns programme, and the minimum space standards for new houses was reduced.

Home ownership had grown in the inter-war years, especially through the rapid expansion of the suburbs around London. After a period of stagnation in the 1940s, it expanded again from the early 1950s onwards. As incomes rose, as a result of high levels of employment and economic growth, home ownership came within reach of a rising section of the population.

Over the past half century there has been a huge growth in the number of owner-occupied homes. As Graph 2.1 indicates, in 1951 there were 3.7 million homeowners. The number increased by 5 million by 1971, and another 5 million by 1991. By 2001 there were 15.6 million households owning their home.

In 2004 70 per cent of households were owner-occupiers. It is a tenure that enables people to have choice over where they live, and a sense of pride and control over their home. For successive generations it has also been a way of obtaining a house with a garden, either in the suburbs or commuter towns and villages. The attractions of home ownership have been increased in a number of different ways.

First, there has been a plentiful supply of finance available
for house purchase, at competitive rates of interest. The well-
established building society movement has been a trustworthy
source of lending, dedicated to enabling people to buy their
own homes. The standard repayment mortgage is structured so
as to spread payments evenly over the life of the mortgage. In
the early years most of the repayments comprise interest on the
outstanding debt, with the capital being repaid only in the later
years.

Second, the benefits of home ownership have also been
strengthened by financial advantages. A key event was the
budget which abolished 'Schedule A tax'. This was a tax based
on the view that owner-occupiers enjoyed a benefit from living
in their property rent free, whereas if they let it they would be
taxed on the rental income. The Schedule A tax was a levy on
this notional – or 'imputed' rent, as it was officially termed –
but to offset this owners were able to claim tax relief on their
mortgage interest payments.

In the 1961 budget the Chancellor of the Exchequer abolished the Schedule A tax, but retained mortgage tax relief. The

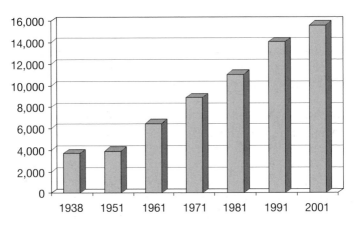

Graph 2.1 Growth in home ownership

change was vehemently opposed by the Labour Party, notably in an eloquent speech by Harold Lever, then Shadow Financial Secretary, in the House of Commons debate on the proposals. However, when the Labour Government came into office three years later it did not reintroduce the tax, but did retain mortgage tax relief.

Those who gained most from tax relief were the owners with the largest mortgages, paying the highest rates of taxation. The annual value of tax relief rose from under £1 billion in 1963/4 to over £9 billion at its peak in 1989/90. For the twenty years from 1974 to 1994, the cost never fell below £4 billion a year. The financial benefits from ownership became almost irresistible to anyone who could get on the first step of the ladder.

Third, house buyers were able to buy homes in the suburbs and rural areas, while local councils were frequently prevented from building homes outside their own boundaries. Residents in the suburbs and settlements beyond the green belt enjoyed the benefits of low densities: detached and semi-detached privately owned houses with gardens, living in neighbourhoods occupied by similar middle class residents and with access to good schools for their children. The local authorities consistently used their political powers to protect the privileges of their electors and to prevent encroachment of rented housing for people wanting to escape from the overcrowded inner city areas.

One example of such resistance to new homes being built was the public inquiry held to consider Manchester's application to build a new town at Lymm in Cheshire in the 1950s. The proposals were strongly opposed by Cheshire County Council, the National Farmers Union and many local interest groups. The Minister decided to reject Manchester's application.[2]

Another failure was the overspill scheme proposed for Westhoughton, fifteen miles from Manchester, which had been suggested as an alternative at the Lymm inquiry in 1957. After long negotiations this was abandoned because agreement could not be reached on a viable site for the development. In the words of a leading planning expert on the history of Manchester overspill: 'the activity has been immense and the results very poor'.[3]

In the West Midlands a celebrated planning inquiry was held in 1959 into Birmingham's proposals for a development of housing for 54,000 people at Wythall, seven miles south of the city on the border between Warwickshire and Worcestershire. There were many objections from landowners and organisations of farmers and residents. Despite voluminous evidence put forward by the City Corporation on the need for overspill caused by the growth of population and slum clearance schemes, Birmingham lost the Wythall inquiry.[4]

In London there has been strenuous resistance over many years to proposals for building housing estates in outer London, although both the London County Council and the Greater London Council were successful in building some estates in both outer London and beyond into the south east. Ken Young and John Kramer have written an exhaustive study of the Greater London Council's efforts to 'open up the suburbs' by increasing opportunities in suburban areas for low-income households. Despite repeated efforts by both Labour and Conservative Government, their efforts largely failed. As the authors conclude: 'The GLC incurred successive defeats . . . in their efforts to secure a more equitable distribution of urban space. Suburban exclusivity was once again guaranteed.'[5]

There have also been numerous examples of hostility to housing developments, where existing communities have campaigned to stop new homes being built. A high profile recent example is the battle that has been waged over plans to build 5,000 new homes on 281 hectares of farmland on the outskirts of Stevenage. The story began in 1997 with investigations by Hertfordshire County Council looking for sites to meet the targets in the revised planning guidance. Following strenuous opposition by local residents in the surrounding villages and local environmental groups, and then by a change in political control to the Conservatives, the County Council withdrew support for the plan. Meanwhile Stevenage Borough Council has strongly supported the development, and lobbied the Government to overrule the County Council. They argue that it would be a 'sustainable urban extension', and not the destruction of the green belt claimed by its opponents.

Among the many instances of opposition to new development, it is important to distinguish between what are legitimate concerns over damage to the environment or inappropriate housing proposals, and what is straightforward selfish opposition to encroachment by newcomers into desirable communities. In practice, making this distinction is not always obvious. Critics almost always seek to argue from the moral high ground of environmental concern, ranging from loss of greenfield land to protection of wildlife and pollution of the environment.

In recent years the resistance to building more housing has grown even stronger as the lobbies for protecting the countryside have become more vocal and organised. Opponents of new development have criticised with some justification the excessive building of large executive homes for long-distance commuters and the failure to build more affordable housing for low-income people. Yet often the underlying argument has been 'Not in my back yard'.

The right to buy

Home ownership was given a huge boost by the 'right to buy' legislation, introduced by Margaret Thatcher's Conservative Government in 1980. The policy was hugely popular with those who benefited and a flagship policy for Mrs Thatcher's new political agenda. Socialism for many people was convincingly portrayed as denying tenants the right to choose the style or colour of their own front door. Frequently, almost the first act after buying was to paint the door in the colour of their choice, as a visible symbol that they were now the owners.

The 'right to buy' provisions have enabled over 2 million tenants to become owners of their homes over the past twenty-five years. The properties sold have disproportionately been the more attractive and popular, especially houses with gardens. Many buyers have been families who would not have been able to afford to buy without the generous discounts. Initially, the value of discounts was 33 per cent, rising by 1 per cent with each year of residence, up to a maximum of 50 per cent. In 1988 the maximum discount for flats was raised to 70 per cent, in order to boost the attractives of buying that type of property.

The right to buy has meant that most people buying their homes have stayed in their existing homes, at least for the five years that is the length of residence required to keep the full discount. This has been important in maintaining a broader income mix on some council-owned housing estates, and preventing those estates providing homes only for those on low incomes. However, when the first buyers have moved out, the dwellings have usually been sold to another owner-occupier, although recently there has been a growth of properties being sold to private landlords. Properties have rarely returned to the stock of socially rented housing. As a result of the right to buy the number of lettings available to local authorities has fallen significantly. Those who have lost out have been existing tenants seeking transfers and people needing a home to rent.

The proceeds from the right to buy have exceeded by far any other form of privatisation. The sale of council homes is one of the few types of privatisation where the policy has been to sell assets at prices far lower than their market value. Properties have been sold to sitting tenants at huge discounts. The total receipts from sales since 1980 now amount to more than £30 billion. The full value of the assets lost to the public sector, however, is double that amount, exceeding £60 billion.

Since 1970 there has been a huge rise in house prices, outstripping the rate of inflation in the economy as whole. In 1970 the average price of a dwelling was £5,000 in the UK. In 1980 this had risen to £24,600, by 1990 to £59,800 and by 2000 to £101,466. The only period of fall came when the housing market collapsed at the end of the 1980s, following a house price boom. In 1989 house prices rose by 21 per cent. Prices fell by almost 10 per cent between 1989 and 1993. In order to afford to buy when house prices were rising, borrowers had been taking out mortgages of up to 100 per cent of the purchase price. At the bottom of the slump 21 per cent of owners were caught in a negative equity trap with the value of their property less than their mortgage liability. There was also a dramatic increase in repossessions, with more than 75,000 homeowners losing their homes in the peak year of 1991. In total more than 300,000 homeowners were repossessed in the five years from 1990 to 1995.

With the exception of that period, there has been an unbroken rise in house prices, especially rapid over the past few years. The increase has caused growing difficulties for first time buyers, especially in London and most other areas of southern England. For existing owners it has led to a huge growth in housing wealth. In 1970 the net equity – the value of the property excluding any outstanding mortgages – possessed by homeowners totalled £36 billion. By 1980 this had risen to £258 billion, by 1990 to £850 billion, by 2000 to £1,432 billion and by 2003 to £2,334 billion.

If the figures are revised to exclude increases resulting from the general level of inflation they still show a massive growth in the value of housing assets.

In 2003 the Treasury and the ODPM commissioned Kate Barker, a member of the Bank of England's Monetary Advisory Committee, to investigate the reasons for the under-supply of housing and the problems of the housing market. Her first report, *Review of Housing Supply*, published in December 2003, documented in detail the failure of housing supply to match housing demand, especially over the past twenty years.[6]

While most previous estimates of housing shortage had focused on meeting housing need, this analysis looked at the effect of housing supply on house prices. In doing this, it challenged the deeply ingrained attitudes that see rising house prices as desirable, because they increase housing wealth and potential spending power.

Among the findings were:

- In 2002 only 37 per cent of new households could afford to buy a home, compared to 46 per cent in the late 1980s.
- As a result of house prices rising by more than the average in other European countries, each first time buyer has paid £32,000 more for their home than elsewhere in Europe.
- Higher house prices have benefited landowners and existing homeowners, but at the expense of younger people seeking homes and the less well-off. The greatest inequality is between homeowners who gain from the rising value of their homes and tenants who get no assets.

One of the most striking findings is that while house prices have risen, in real terms, by an average of 3.3 per cent a year in the UK between 1971 and 2001, in France they have risen by an average of 1.1 per cent and in Germany by a mere 0.1 per cent. This is primarily due to greater housing supply matching the growth in households. The effect of the near zero inflation of house prices in Germany is that the ratio of house prices to income has fallen by 30 per cent over the past thirty years. This has had a marked impact in making home ownership and market rents affordable to a wider range of households.

The growth of home ownership has brought many benefits to the great majority of people who have bought their homes. It is the tenure of choice for most people who can afford to buy, except younger people who do not expect to stay in the same accommodation for more than a short period and prefer to rent from a private landlord. As well as the benefits of being able to choose where to live, and being able to decide on any improvements and extensions, most homeowners benefited for many years from mortgage tax relief, and almost all have gained from the rising value of their capital assets.

It is important to recognise all these benefits, but also to understand how some of the opportunities for people buying their homes have reduced choice for people wanting a home to rent and widened inequalities between owners and renters.

Chapter 3

The mass housing disaster

The problem.

Council housing

Between 1950 and 1980 local authorities built more than three million homes. At the end of this period 30 per cent of all households were renting from local councils. Yet council housing was not seen as a success story. Its growing band of critics saw municipal ownership of rented housing as the problem, not the solution.

The single most significant reason for this loss of popularity of council housing was the quality of the high-density flatted estates that were built. At the start of the 1950s the major cities were faced with a massive problem, as they tried to replace the homes that had been destroyed in the war, demolish the dilapidated nineteenth-century slums and to find accommodation for the growing number of young families.

From the mid 1950s public housing experienced a revolution, as blocks of flats replaced the earlier emphasis on building houses with gardens. The 'clean sweep' vision of the planners saw no future for the tightly knit streets of terraced housing. The construction firms wanted large contracts for their new 'mass housing' systems of industrialised building. Governments of both parties, seduced by the prospect of mass housing on the cheap actively urged the new systems on local authorities.

At the peak of the public housing programme more than half of the properties built were flats. In 1968, 88,600 flats were approved in England and Wales.[1] In total almost 200,000 flats of ten storeys and more were built in England. They were heavily concentrated in the major cities – Liverpool, Manchester, Sheffield and Newcastle and over a third were built in London, where at the peak of the boom 47 per cent of new rented homes were high-rise.[2]

High-rise building received higher amounts of public subsidy. The new subsidy introduced in 1955 was structured according to the height of the building, so that flats in five storey blocks got more than twice the subsidy as that given for houses, and flats in fifteen storey blocks or more got nearly three times as much. The market for high-rise construction was dominated by seven major companies, and most strongly by George Wimpey, John Laing and Taylor Woodrow. Between 1963 and 1973 these firms were responsible for three quarters of all industrialised high-rise developments.[3]

Industrialised building techniques were also adopted for many of the medium-rise flats, including deck access flats such as the 2,400 dwelling Aylesbury estate in Southwark, which was reported at the time to be the largest housing contract ever let. Some estates of this type became the most notorious public housing disasters.

Another driver of the policy for high-density, industrialised building programme was the unexpected rise in the population, as the birth rate soared in the early 1950s and the number of households grew as young people left home earlier to start their families.

The concept of *urban containment* was a key element in the post-war planning vision. The policies included restricting unplanned urban sprawl and preventing building on green belt land. It commanded widespread political, professional and public support for the social and environmental benefits it promised. What it also meant was that inner city local authorities had no option but to build most new rented homes at high densities within their own boundaries. Beleaguered by the pressures from thousands of families wanting re-housing, hemmed in by political resistance to building council houses in the middle class suburbs, and bribed by a subsidy system biased towards high-rise development, too many local authorities uncritically accepted the new building systems.

Park Hill, Sheffield

J. L. Womersley and Architectural Press

There were some who embraced the new approach enthusiastically because they believed that the old terraced houses were too small and inflexible for modern families, and that the new estates would offer more space and a wider mix of dwellings. Some of these had been influenced by early examples of high-rise developments, such as the highly publicised new housing development at Roehampton, designed by the London County Council architects team. These homes benefited not only from high quality design, but also spacious green areas surrounding the flats. Unfortunately, the high-rise, systems-built redevelopment schemes on inner city sites were very different.

The merits of industrialised housing never matched the promises made for it. As Alison Ravetz has said 'Design faults, skimped workmanship and inadequate supervision were hugely magnified by the scale of contracts. High-rise dwellings so constructed were particularly prone to damp and mould, and the electric heating systems were often ineffective and hugely expensive to run.'[4]

Even the advocates of high-rise flats recognised that they were not suitable for families with young children. Yet in practice many such families were re-housed in those blocks, with predictable results of young children being cooped up inside the flats because their parents understandably and reasonably were not willing to let them out on their own.

The estimates for slum clearance were at best crude guesses, with extraordinary inconsistencies in the figures. Some authorities in the old northern conurbations reported that over a third of all dwellings in their areas were unfit, while adjacent authorities had the same number of unfit dwellings as councils in leafy suburbs. In most areas no inspections had been carried out to assess the properties. Certainly the tenants who lived in the properties had not been consulted on whether they believed that demolition was the only sensible solution.

A devastating critique by Raphael Samuel exposed the flaws in the estimates. His article showed that 'the recorded percentage of unfit houses was the same in Carshalton as in St. Pancras, in Penge as in Hammersmith, rather higher in Sunbury-on-Thames than in Islington, and twice as high in Rickmansworth as in Hackney. Sutton and Cheam actually returned more slum houses than Stoke Newington, as did Potters Bar, Wimbledon, Finchley and Elstree'. [5]

A scrutiny of the statistics should have led Ministers and officials to reject them as virtually worthless. However, they were used for years – as unchallengeable facts – as the basis for a housing policy which would cause massive upheavals in the lives of millions of people, transform the character of almost all British cities and burden a future generation with an unwelcome housing legacy.

What should have been recognised was that the problems were far more complex and diverse than labelling dwellings as 'unfit' and demolishing them. Undoubtedly there were old properties whose condition was beyond renovation at any reasonable cost. There were many more in the clearance programmes where the installation of inside toilets, baths, better heating and thorough structural repairs could have turned them into homes with many years of useful life ahead. Especially in inner London some houses that escaped the bulldozer were improved by incoming owner-occupiers and today are much desired expensive homes.

Some of the desperate housing problems people experienced were not mainly due to the physical condition of the properties. The scarcity of cheaper rented housing forced many families, especially newly arrived migrants, to live in seriously over-crowded one or two room flats, often sharing with several other tenants. Some unscrupulous landlords exploited the shortage to charge exorbitant rents. The 1957 Rent Act removed secur-ity of tenure on new lettings and allowed landlords to evict – or threaten to evict – any tenants who complained about conditions.

In the areas covered by the clearance programmes many tenants failed to get re-housing by the council, especially newer arrivals in furnished tenancies who were not deemed eligible. Tenants who moved in after clearance plans had been decided by the council were not entitled to re-housing. Landlords often evicted tenants, in the hope they would get more money from the council if it was sold with vacant possession. Predictably it was the newer arrivals, especially the migrants coming from the black Commonwealth countries in the late 1950s and early 1960s, who were most frequently excluded or evicted as a result of racial discrimination.

As the need to re-house tenants from the area to be cleared was given priority, fewer applicants could be re-housed from the local authority housing waiting lists. So as sharing and over-crowding got worse in the neighbourhoods not covered by the clearance programmes, so did the prospects of being re-housed by the council. It was a vicious circle.

The policy of building large, systems-built housing estates had devastating consequences. Instead of houses with gardens that most people aspired to – the 'Bevan' houses of the early post-war years – tenants were forced to live in bleak tower blocks and deck access flats. They did not see the new flats as realising their housing dream, but as a disappointing second best for

 what tr. avoid

people with no other choice. It is hard to see the utopian vision of Unwin's early council housing in many of the estates which were built in those years.

Through the 1950s and 1960s there was huge pressure to clear the slums and meet the housing needs of a rising population. Which political party would build – or had built – most homes was a major issue at every General Election. The number of new homes built reached its peak of 370,000 in 1968. Ironically, this same year saw the dramatic physical collapse of Ronan Point in Canning Town in east London. On 15 May 1968 a gas explosion blew out the load-bearing wall on the flat of Mrs Ivy Hodge, the tenant on the eighteenth floor of the block of flats. A progressive collapse brought every living room crashing on top of the one below. Four tenants died, with another 11 injured. It was a human tragedy which came to symbolise the collapse of confidence in that form of housing development.[6]

During the twenty years from the mid 1950s almost 1.5 million dwellings were demolished: one in ten of all the homes in the country. The new homes had more space and better amenities than the dwellings they replaced. There were dramatic reductions in the number of homes without a bath, hot water or inside WC; people sharing facilities in multi-occupied houses; families living at densities of more than one and a half persons to a room; and in properties designated as 'unfit for human habitation'.[7]

Yet a high price was paid for these gains. When the old neighbourhoods of houses, shops and small businesses were razed to the ground, they were replaced by monolithic single tenure estates of council flats, many in high-rise or long deck access blocks. Amid all the powerful pressures, there was little room for the choices and aspirations of tenants to be heard.

destroyed organic community

Failings in housing management

After the First World War, local authorities had been chosen as the agents for providing most new 'housing for the working classes'. With isolated exceptions, no significant role in building

Ronan Point, Canning Town, 1968

Popperfoto

new homes was played by the charitable housing trusts founded in the late nineteenth century.

In most local authorities, housing responsibilities were split between several departments – building works, treasurers, housing management, sanitary inspectors and for some larger authorities also architects. As rents were too high for poorly paid workers or the unemployed, most male tenants were in skilled manual or clerical jobs. Most properties were self-contained houses. Once the homes were built, little was expected from the council except collecting the rent and arranging for any repairs needed. The fragmentation of housing management responsibility was not a serious problem. However, it left local authorities unprepared for the role they were soon to be expected to play in the massive programme of slum clearance and redevelopment. There was no body of shared professional knowledge and expertise and few high calibre senior managers.

Managing large estates of high-rise and deck access flats was very different. If lifts broke down tenants faced walking up numerous flights of stairs, and elderly or disabled tenants could be trapped in their flats. Entry phone systems could easily be vandalised. Entrance areas and staircases were vulnerable to being daubed with graffiti, or more seriously to physical attacks on vulnerable residents. Communal areas around blocks of flats could become dumping grounds for unwanted furniture, broken-down vehicles, bags of rubbish and litter. Unless such areas were adequately lit, many tenants were afraid to leave their flats after dark.

The problems of high-density flatted estates were not unique to Britain. Anne Power has written a fascinating study of mass housing estates in northern Europe, which describes the experiences of estates in France, Germany, Denmark and Ireland, as well as Britain.[8]

Management problems emerged on many of the new estates soon after they were completed. Where the problems were not tackled the estates with the worst problems embarked on a spiral of decline. By the 1970s the phenomenon of 'hard to let' estates emerged as a growing problem, even in areas with long council waiting lists. In a small number of urban housing authorities the problems escalated out of control. The number of empty properties grew, rent arrears increased and repair backlogs built up, even for urgent repairs. Staff morale plummeted. Tenants felt disempowered and became increasingly angry.

Not surprisingly those who were already hostile to council housing seized on these problems. In the mid 1970s the Conservative Party was becoming increasingly critical of what it saw as the excessive power of the state. Council housing was a prime target. Politicians ignored the role that an earlier Conservative Government had played in the promotion of high-density housing estates and untested industry building systems, and launched virulent attacks on the incompetence of Labour-controlled local authorities. Many of the criticisms of high-density, systems-built flats and the failure of local authority management were fully justified, but it is also important to recognise that there was a deep, class-based animosity to council housing which had been displayed from its early years, as shown by the long battle over the Cutteslowe wall described in Chapter 1 and the resistance to building new council homes outside the boundaries of the urban areas.

lack of maintenance causes for breakdown

Chapter 4

The changing nature of rented housing

The fortunes of private renting

In 1900 over 90 per cent of people in Britain rented their homes privately, ranging from the rich to the poor. In that year 150,000 new homes were built in this country, almost all by private landlords. But even before the outbreak of the First World War the number of new homes being built fell sharply – to a level of only 50,000 in 1913.

The cause of the decline was a combination of more attractive opportunities for capital investment and a falling demand for new homes. As the famous Rowntree poverty studies shockingly showed there were millions of people living in squalid and overcrowded dwellings – the problem was that they lacked the money to pay the rents for better homes.

During the inter-war period private landlords, whose prospective returns were limited by rent control and who were given no help from public subsidy, played only a small role. The years immediately following the Second World War followed a similar pattern and saw even fewer homes built by private landlords.

The critical watershed was the 1957 Rent Act, which led to bitter controversy over rent de-control and security of tenure, and made privately rented housing a battleground between landlords and tenants and between political parties for the next thirty years. For the supporters of the Act, it restored the hope that private landlords could be encouraged to reverse the decline and help in meeting the housing shortage by encouraging more landlords to let out properties – with the expectation of a reasonable return on their investment. For its critics the activities of Rachman and other rogue landlords confirmed their direst warnings, showing how unscrupulous landlords could harass and exploit vulnerable tenants.

In 1965 the Labour Government brought in the Rent Act which restored security of tenure to unfurnished tenants and limited the rent that landlords could charge to 'fair rents' set by an independent Rent Office. However, the Act did not include furnished tenancies, and, in the years that followed, landlords used this loophole to let a high proportion of new tenancies in this way. A succession of reports – such as the Notting Hill Housing Survey of 1968 – showed how furnished tenants were paying higher rents for less room, and how the sector was disproportionately occupied by more recently arrived immigrants from the black Commonwealth who were denied access to unfurnished lettings. In inner London especially, a rising number of tenants were applying to councils because they were facing homelessness through eviction from furnished flats. Following persistent lobbying by housing campaigners, tenants groups and MPs, the Labour Government brought in the 1974 Rent Act, which restored security of tenure to furnished tenants of non-resident landlords and brought them within the 'fair rent' regime of the 1965 Act.

Throughout this period controls on rents and powers to evict were strongly opposed by landlords' organisations and Conservative politicians on the grounds they were harming those who most needed homes to rent. What the evidence shows is that the fall in private tenancies was consistently around 100,000 a year from the end of the 1950s to the late 1980s, throughout all the changes in the Rent Acts from de-control and back.

The most plausible explanation is that the reluctance of landlords to let was influenced by factors outside the Rent Acts, most importantly the benefits of home ownership. Owner-occupiers were entitled to mortgage tax relief, whereas private landlords were not, and the high interest rates that prevailed during this period further increased the value of tax relief.

Anyone who could afford a mortgage was better-off buying. While high inflation rapidly reduced the real costs of mortgage payments, rents continued to rise with inflation. Renting was attractive only for tenants paying rents below market levels as a result of rent control, people wanting a tenancy for a short period only and tenants whose accommodation came with their job. Almost everyone else seeking privately rented homes did so simply because it was their only option – they could not afford to buy and were unable to obtain accommodation from a council or housing association.

In 1988 the Conservative Government at last took action to remove the restrictions on market rents and the rights of tenants to security that they had consistently opposed. The 1988 Housing Act maintained protection for existing tenants, but allowed landlords to let all new tenancies at market rents and on assured short hold tenancies, which could be for periods of six months renewable at the discretion of the landlord.

The results were strikingly different from the Rent Act thirty years earlier. There was an increase of over half a million tenancies in the years following the Act, an increase of 30 per cent. As house prices collapsed, hundreds of thousands of homeowners were trapped in negative equity and repossessions soared to a peak of over 80,000 a year. Many former owners had no option but to rent. Younger people became more hesitant about buying their home. Many landlords chose to continue renting out their properties when they became vacant.

Over the past forty years there have been major changes in the people who rent from private landlords and the reasons why they do so. In 1965 the private rented sector was suffering from many years of little investment and low maintenance. Conditions were worse than in any other tenure – more unfit properties, more overcrowding, more multi-occupation and more properties lacking a bath, hot water or inside toilet. Landlords had little incentive to improve their property. Most tenants rented from a private landlord not from choice, but because they had no alternative.

Since the 1977 Homeless Persons Act local authorities have had legal duties to secure accommodation for those homeless households who are in priority need. One important consequence when those groups become homeless is that they no longer need to search for somewhere to live in the privately rented sector, in order to avoid ending up on the streets, face separation from their partners or have their children taken into care. They have a legal right to accommodation from their local council.

Changes in social housing

Until the end of the 1960s tenants from a wide range of incomes occupied council and housing association accommodation. Over the next twenty years the profile of social housing tenants changed dramatically, and by the end of the 1980s most households renting from social landlords did not have a member with an earned income.

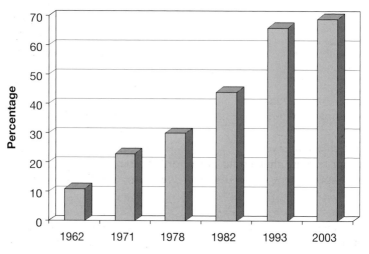

Graph 4.1 Percentage of local authority tenants with no earner (1962–2003)

There were three different factors that led to this change. The first was that access to council housing was opened up to more low-income groups, who had previously been excluded or under-represented. The second was the change in the income levels of existing tenants, with an increase in the number of households without anyone in paid employment. The third factor was that better-off tenants were leaving the council housing sector.

The Conservative Government's 1972 Housing Finance Act required local authorities to set up a rent rebate scheme for all tenants. Prior to the legislation any rebate schemes had been discretionary. The Act made them mandatory. Prior to this legislation low wage earners were not entitled to any help in meeting their housing costs. Only those receiving supplementary benefit through the social security system received financial help in paying their rents. In 1982 rent rebates were replaced by housing benefit through the Social Security and Housing Benefits Act.

A main objective of the Housing Finance Act was to remove the freedom of local authorities to decide on the level of rents. The view of the Government was that many local authorities, especially Labour-controlled authorities, were charging rents that were too low. The Act compelled them to charge 'fair rents', which in most areas were higher than the previous rents. The new provisions for rebates were designed to enable people on lower wages to pay the higher rents.

From the earliest days of the philanthropic housing trusts better-off working class families mainly occupied the new homes. As shown earlier, the rents charged by the Peabody Trust were too high for the poorest families. They benefited the 'artisan', not the 'labourer'. Many of the poorest families lived in one room because they could not afford the rents of larger accommodation.[1] Seebohm Rowntree made similar findings in his studies of poverty in York.[2]

Similarly the rents charged for the first council homes were too high for less skilled workers or non-earning households. *Working Class Wives*, published in 1938 was a study based on interviews and surveys of 1,250 married women. It recorded the multiple difficulties they experienced caused by poverty, bad housing, overcrowding, poor diet and sheer exhaustion. Many families were forced to accept bad housing simply because they could not afford anything better.[3]

One woman in Battersea in south London had a family of eight, living in two rooms, sharing a lavatory with sixteen others. The rent was 7s 6d. She couldn't afford council rents at 19s 7d per week, because when her husband was out of work they only had an income of 33s 3d a week.[4]

The rents were too high for poor families on the estates built after the Second World War, especially for newly built houses with gardens. Over the years some authorities had sought to house tenants on low wages by keeping rents as low as possible, and subsidising council homes from their rate fund as well as the central government subsidies they received. The removal of their power to do this was what made the 1972 Act so hugely controversial.

The increase in the number of tenants receiving rebates was spectacular, exceeding by far the projections of take-up. In 1972, before the new Act came into force, 272,000 tenants were receiving rebates from discretionary local authority schemes. By 1976 the number receiving rebates had soared to 945,000. Together with over a million tenants receiving supplementary benefit, this meant that 44 per cent of all tenants were paying less than the full rent.[5] The 1972 Act broke the link between income and access to good quality housing for people on low incomes. The result was that more low-income households were able to take up council and housing association tenancies, especially where higher rents were charged.

Another important factor was the allocation policies of local authorities. Even when rents were affordable by those on a low income many local councils had been reluctant to house families who were regarded as 'feckless'.

Another type of exclusion was racial discrimination. Following the post-war arrival of large number of immigrants from black Commonwealth countries, many local authorities pursued discriminatory lettings policies.

Studies of inner city areas, such as Sparkbrook in Birmingham and Notting Hill in London, found large numbers of low-income households renting rooms in run-down multi-occupied properties from private landlords. Whole families had to live in just one room, and these included a disproportionate number of black tenants. Many had been unable to obtain council housing because of lengthy residence requirements and rules which penalised tenants in furnished accommodation, which many black tenants occupied.

In 1969 an influential report, *Council Housing: Purposes, Procedures and Priorities* was published by the Government's Central Housing Advisory Committee, chaired by Professor Barry Cullingworth.[6] It recommended that local councils should remove restrictions on eligibility for council housing, such as long periods of residence in the area, and end personal councillor involvement in allocation decisions. There was considerable evidence that these practices had discriminated against racial minorities, who were under-represented in council housing, despite experiencing the worst housing conditions. Although the recommendations were not mandatory, the Government actively endorsed the recommendations and many local councils changed their allocation policies to give greater priority to housing need.

Changes to the treatment of homeless people were also an important factor on the make-up of social housing tenants. The only legal duty towards people who became homeless until 1977 had been a clause in the 1948 National Assistance Act. Under this Act the welfare departments of local authorities were required to help homeless people who were in urgent need – 'destitute' as defined in the legislation – but only through the provision of temporary accommodation.

Accommodation for families had typically been in emergency hostels, often admitting only mothers and their children, with residents forced to share bathrooms, toilets and cooking facilities. The fathers were expected to fend for themselves. Not surprisingly, homeless families applied only as the very last resort when every other attempt to find even temporary shelter had failed.

The way homeless families could be treated was dramatically portrayed in the 1966 BBC TV documentary *Cathy Come Home*, with its moving story of a family being broken up through the experience of becoming homeless. Although there had been no joint planning, Shelter, the national campaign for homeless people, was launched ten days later, with huge media coverage, and its high profile campaigning raised public and political concern over the treatment of homeless families.

In 1968 the influential Seebohm report on the future organisation of social services recommended that homelessness should be treated as the responsibility of housing departments, not the new social service departments (which incorporated the old welfare departments). In 1974 a Government Circular was issued accepting this. This was an important recognition that homelessness should be recognised as a *housing* problem, rather than simply a *welfare* problem, but the Government advice had no statutory force.

The more progressive local authorities accepted the recommendations to provide long-term permanent housing for homeless applicants. Many councils did not, and several thousand children a year were being taken into care because their families were homeless. In response there was a sustained campaign by voluntary organisations to place a legal duty on local authorities to provide accommodation for homeless families. The campaign was led by Shelter and SHAC, then the leading London housing advice centre, particularly its Director, Nick Raynsford (who twenty years later was the Housing Minister who introduced the 2002 Homelessness Bill in Parliament). The outcome was the 1977 Homeless Persons Act, introduced as a Private Members Bill by the Liberal MP, Stephen Ross, but supported by the Labour Government.

For the first time local housing authorities were under a *legal duty* to provide accommodation to homeless families and vulnerable single people. They were no longer able, legally, to refuse to house people because they judged they would be 'bad tenants' or were 'undeserving'.

Sixty years earlier the 1919 Housing Act had become law, placing for the first time a duty on local authorities to build homes in order to tackle the housing shortage. The 1977 Homeless Persons Act was a new landmark, with its duty on local authorities to secure accommodation for homeless applicants because of the severity of housing need.

In the first year after the Act came into force 50,000 households were accepted by local councils as being homeless and in priority need of accommodation. Almost all were re-housed directly into council tenancies. During the next decade the number of homeless applicants rose sharply, so that in 1990 local authorities accepted over 90,000 homeless households. The effect of the legislation was to increase significantly the number of families in acute housing being re-housed into council housing. Those accepted as homeless included many house-holds on low incomes, especially single parents dependent on welfare support.

During the 1980s there was also a massive increase in unemployment as a result of the upheavals in economy, particulary huge job losses in the old manufacturing, coal and shipbuilding industries, companies forced into liquidation and staff declared redundant. As a result, the proportion of council tenants in employment fell sharply.

The number of tenants receiving rent rebates rose sharply during the 1970s and 1980s, especially as a result of the increase in unemployment. In 1974, immediately after the introduction of the statutory rent rebate scheme, the number of tenants receiving direct rebates or supplementary benefit was 1,974,000. In 1984 the number of tenants receiving either standard or certificated housing benefit (which had replaced the previous schemes) was 3,125,000.[7] During the early 1990s there was a further rise in the numbers of council and housing association tenants receiving housing benefit as a result of the sharp rise in housing association rents. The percentage of social housing tenants receiving help with their rents rose from 42 to 44 per cent in the late 1970s and from 66 to 67 per cent in the mid 1990s.[8]

Moving out of council housing

The profile of council housing tenants was also changed by people moving out of council housing as a result of dissatisfaction with their homes or their neighbourhood.

Many of the early council housing estates were models of good quality planning and design. Conditions enjoyed by the tenants were vastly better than the overcrowded tenements from which they had escaped. From the 1950s, however, the quality of new estates fell, first through lower space standards and then through the building of high-density badly designed blocks of flats. At first many tenants were glad to accept almost anything to escape from the run-down, ill-equipped places where they had been living. Over time it became clear that where they were able to move out many tenants would do so.

A study of levels of dissatisfaction with different types of neighbourhood has found that the highest levels of dissatisfaction of all types of housing are on inner city estates, especially in London, in high-rise housing, and in deprived industrial areas.[9] The worst problems are on poor-quality estates, where high levels of crime, failing schools, bad housing and a poor reputation all combine. It is in these areas that almost everyone who can get out does so. In 1998, the Social Exclusion Unit estimated that there were more than one million households living in these neighbourhoods.[10]

The difficulties in these areas are frequently described as 'the problem' of social housing: that it houses too many poor tenants, too many vulnerable people, and that too much priority is given to housing need. Those who put the problem in this way are making a fundamental mistake. The problem is not that people who are poor live in social housing. It is that they are too often all housed together on the same estates.

Ironically, in the light of later experience, the early council housing was built as estates because that form of layout was seen as superior to the traditional urban streets, which were associated with congestion and squalor. The visionary pioneers of council housing saw it as a model for the future. Yet homes need not have continued to be built in single tenure estates as they came to be occupied predominantly by poorer tenants. It would have been possible to build estates with a mix of owner-occupied and rented homes. It would also have been possible for councils to provide homes for rent by buying vacant properties on the private market, in the way that many people buying their home choose to do, and as housing associations started to do in the 1960s.

It is also important to stress that despite the problems, council housing is not, and should not be portrayed as, a picture of unremitting gloom. Especially in small towns and villages most council homes are well-designed, attractive properties, built in small terraces or as semi-detached houses, and an integral part of the fabric of those communities. Surveys show that almost 70 per cent of council tenants say they are satisfied with their homes, although the percentage has been falling in the last few years.

However, some better-off tenants would have left council housing anyway, even if the mistakes, which have been described, had not occurred. During the 1980s almost a million tenants bought their homes, taking advantage of the right to buy, with its very generous discounts. Those who bought were the better-off tenants, many whose grown-up children had left home and were no longer financially dependent on their parents. However, this has been only one factor in the growth of home ownership. Surveys consistently show that most people aspire to own their home, and rising living standards have brought this within the reach of most people in work. It is without doubt the tenure of choice.

Rising owner-occupation is not a new phenomenon. Home ownership grew rapidly in the inter-war years, as large numbers of lower middle class and skilled working class families took advantage of falling house prices and bought homes in the suburbs. It expanded again from the 1950s, with mortgage tax relief becoming an important incentive.

High levels of home ownership are a consistent feature in all advanced societies. However, despite the fall in the number of council homes, the UK has a larger proportion of socially rented housing than most European countries, and significantly higher than the US.

These different events and policy changes – the housing benefit assistance, changes in local authority lettings policies, homeless legislation, the increase in unemployment and the right to buy – have had a cumulative effect on the composition of the group who rented from social landlords. The scale of the change was dramatic. In 1978 the average income of council tenants was 73 per cent of the national average. By 1990 this had fallen to 48 per cent. Council housing has become a tenure occupied predominantly by the poor.[11] See Graph 4.1, p. 44.

A study of social rented housing across different European countries found that households with the lowest 20 per cent of incomes were more likely to be found in social housing in Britain than in France, the Netherlands or Germany, and that this may be due to the much greater importance attached to social rented housing as a safety net in Britain compared to other countries. The researchers comment that:

> A more socially mixed social rented sector may arise from the exclusion of vulnerable households from the sector. In some countries social landlords are reluctant to house the most deprived households, for financial or social reasons.[12]

The changing composition of social housing is now frequently described as the 'residualisation of council housing'. It is important to be clear what is meant by the use of this term. It can be used in reference to the falling number of people living in council housing, but the more appropriate issue is the total number of people in all forms of socially rented housing. This has declined, but at 20 per cent still comprises a very substantial share of the population.

The term residualisation is also used in reference to council housing, in particular, having become a tenure of 'last resort'.

If this is made as a negative comment, it is profoundly misguided. It should be seen as a positive development that socially rented housing now accommodates more people who were in severe housing need and people who are vulnerable. Despite the demands this makes, social landlords are far better able to house and support vulnerable people than private landlords, and should see it as their role to do so.

The under-representation of the poorest and the exclusion of people in the greatest need was a significant failure in the past, and the policy changes which remedied that, should be strongly welcomed. What is too often a real failure is the lack of adequate support for vulnerable tenants, in helping them to sustain their tenancy successfully and in mediating where there are conflicts with neighbours.

What is a serious cause of concern is the huge difference that now exists between owners and renters. There is physical segregation, with most owners living in low-density suburbs or rural communities, and many tenants living in high-density urban estates, and differences in the quality of homes and the desirability of neighbourhoods are substantial. Homeowners are able to choose where they live, while most tenants enjoy little choice. There has been a growing divide in the ownership of capital assets, so that this has become one of the major causes of inequality in Britain.

It is not possible to turn the clock back to a 'golden age' of council housing. Even if it were possible, we should remember that it was a golden age only for the more fortunate. Social housing will be a minority tenure in the future and almost all of those who can afford to will choose to buy. More controversially it means accepting that social housing is, and should be, the tenure of 'last resort'. That means not only giving priority to those in the greatest need who have no other option, but also that exclusion is only acceptable in carefully defined and exceptional circumstances.

Renting from a social landlord is a second choice for most tenants, but that does not mean tenants cannot have good quality, well-managed homes, where they can take pride in where they live. They can have choice, within the constraints of cost and supply, but not those arbitrarily imposed by paternalism or lack of imagination. The inequality between owners and tenants can and should be reduced, especially in enabling tenants to share the benefits of building up capital assets. The proposals in the following chapters will also show how there are solutions which would break the identification of 'social housing' with 'housing estates' and re-shape it in a more diverse and attractive form.

Chapter 5

Managing social housing

By the 1980s council housing was facing serious problems. In many urban areas the era of mass housing construction had left local authorities with high-density estates, which were difficult to manage and increasingly unpopular with tenants. The Conservative Government favoured new homes for rent being built by housing associations. It had virtually stopped building by local councils, and was looking for new ways of ending local authority ownership of rented housing.

The right to buy was proving even more popular than expected. Yet tenants on low incomes could not afford to buy, and there were still more than three million tenants renting from councils. If the Government wanted to end local authority housing, an alternative was needed.

The first idea was to give tenants the right to opt out of council ownership. The 1988 Housing Act included provisions that enabled tenants to vote for an alternative landlord, chosen by the tenants. If a majority of tenants on an estate voted in favour, the local authority was legally required to sell the properties to the new landlord.

Believing that many tenants were profoundly disillusioned with their councils as landlords, the Government hoped for an enthusiastic response to their new policies. They were disappointed. The policy was a spectacular failure. Still more embarrassing for the Government was the character of the only group of tenants who chose to take advantage of the legislation.

In north Paddington a group of tenants had been organising a high profile campaign against plans by Westminster City Council to sell their homes to a private developer. When the 1988 Housing Act became law they decided to use the new powers to force the council to sell the estate to their own resident-controlled association, Walterton and Elgin Community Homes (WECH).

When the option was put to the ballot, the tenants and leaseholders voted overwhelmingly to take over ownership. The council was furious, but powerless to stop the sale. Worse still, when the District Valuer assessed the value of the properties and the cost of bringing them up to a satisfactory condition, he calculated that the council must pay a 'dowry' of £26 million to WECH to enable them to carry out the redevelopment and renovation (see also Chapter 11).

Thwarted in this attempt to 'liberate' council tenants from the fiefdom of municipal ownership, the Government turned to the option of transfers to housing associations.

The rising star of housing associations

Following the First World War, local authorities became almost the sole providers of new socially rented housing. The nineteenth-century philanthropic housing associations had been the pioneers of housing for working class tenants, but after the First World War the responsibility for building new rented homes was given to local authorities and the role of housing associations became marginal. A few new housing associations were formed in the inter-war years, and some of the old trusts continued to build new estates, but their total output was small. In the period following the Second World War only a small number of housing associations continued to develop.

In the early 1960s, however, a new wave of housing associations emerged. The best known was the Notting Hill Housing Trust, set up by a charismatic Church of Scotland minister, Rev. Bruce Kenrick.[1] To raise money to buy its first houses, the Trust placed fundraising appeals with photos of a family with six children sharing a single room, and was overwhelmed by the generous response. Similar associations were set up in Glasgow, Liverpool and Birmingham as well as other areas of inner London.

The main activity of the newly formed associations was to buy up run-down street properties and convert them into self-contained flats for low-income families. Despite the lack of adequate public subsidies the new associations developed into an influential lobby.

The 1974 Housing Act marked two major changes in housing policy. The plans for Housing Action Areas (HAAs) gave local authorities new powers to secure the renovation of areas of run-down older property, where policies for voluntary improvement had either not been effective or had resulted in the displacement of low-income tenants. Housing associations were expected to play an important role in acquiring and renovating properties where private landlords were unwilling to do so.

The new legislative arrangements for housing associations had three elements. During the 1960s a number of surveyors, lawyers and other professionals, who were earning fees for the work they were doing, set up housing associations. The powers for registering associations were designed to exclude associations run by fee-earning professionals from receiving public subsidies. The financial provisions for housing associations introduced unexpectedly generous capital and revenue subsidies. To fund the development of more homes the Housing Corporation was given a massively enhanced budget, both for new build and renovation. Between 1975 and 1980 approvals were given for an average of almost 40,000 new homes a year.

Approximately half this programme was spent on the renovation of older properties, especially in inner city areas. Housing associations played a leading role in many HAAs, as well as the earlier General Improvement Areas (GIAs), by buying up both vacant properties and properties that private landlords were not able or willing to improve. As a result of this activity there was a remarkable transformation in many older neighbourhoods.

The election of the Conservative Government in 1979 marked a major change in housing policy. The top priority was the encouragement of home ownership, with the right-to-buy provisions being the flagship for the new Tory approach. More money was allocated to shared ownership schemes, and funding for local councils and housing associations in providing rented homes suffered successive cuts. It became increasingly difficult for housing associations to sustain the inner city renovation programmes that had been so successful in the earlier decade.

Building new homes for rent by local councils was virtually ended. Although housing associations were funded to build new homes, the total number of new homes built for rent by local councils and housing associations averaged only 50,000 in the 1980s, compared to over 120,000 in the 1970s and more than 200,000 in the peak years of the 1960s.

The 1988 Housing Act was a turning point for housing associations. The Government had become increasingly concerned about the high cost of housing association capital subsidies. The Government's aim was to fund more of the cost of housing association development through private finance, and to reduce the dependence on public funding. To maintain their development programmes housing associations had to borrow from private lenders.

Following the 1988 Act total capital expenditure by housing associations rose sharply, from £1 billion in 1988/9 to a peak of £3.6 billion in 1992/3. It then fell progressively each year to £1.9 million in 1997/8. Despite this reduction, however, the level of capital spending was £1 billion a year higher as a result of the injection of private finance.

Housing associations were now seen as a credible alternative to council housing. They had shown their ability to both develop and manage socially rented housing, and were seen as more efficient and more responsive landlords than local authority housing departments. The Government decided it wanted housing associations to take on a much bigger role. The aim was to transfer the existing stock of council housing to either newly formed or existing housing associations.

However, in order to give transfers democratic legitimacy, it was recognised that they should only take place with the support of a majority of tenants in a formal ballot and after tenants had been circulated with a detailed prospectus outlining the proposals. The prospectus was required to include information on rents for the next five years, and proposals for major works to the housing stock.

By 2003 111 local authorities had transferred all their stock to housing associations, comprising 643,000 tenanted homes. Over 23 local authorities had transferred part of their stock, comprising 72,000 homes. Where stock has been transferred the vast majority has been taken into ownership by newly created, rather than existing housing associations. The breakdown of ownership showed that transfer housing associations owned 18.9 per cent, non-transfer associations 19.5 per cent, and 63.6 per cent was still with local authorities. Although more than 100 local authorities no longer had a direct landlord role, 245 councils retained ownership of their housing stock.[2]

Hal Pawson and Cathie Fancy have studied what differences the stock transfer process has made, basing their findings on interviews with participants and comparisons of performance data. Their overall conclusions were positive:

> Since the late 1980s stock transfer has been a catalyst for substantial change in the delivery of social housing services and in the management of social housing organisations. In part, this reflects the ability of transfer associations to access investment resources, but also derives from the fact that the post-transfer regime has tended to result in:
>
> - a liberating effect on housing staff
> - the adoption of a more customer-focused approach to housing management
> - innovation in landlords' organisational structures and staff management practice in favour of more openness and more widespread ownership of corporate objectives.
>
> Transfer often triggers a genuine transformation in organisational ethos – summarised by staff interviewees in some of our case studies as replacing a 'no' culture with a 'yes' culture.[3]

However, when a detailed analysis of performance data was made the results of stock transfer associations and local authorities were remarkably similar. Contrary to the widespread view among government ministers and civil servants, the evidence does not show that stock transfer landlords are more efficient than local authorities, although they do compare favourably with other housing associations.

> Stakeholder views chime with previous research showing that housing management performance (and average tenant satisfaction) tends to improve following stock transfer. There is, however, no clear evidence for the belief that transfer housing associations, as a class of landlords, outperform comparable local authorities.
>
> While transfer landlords may be more tenant-influenced, more tenant friendly and consumerist in outlook, it is not clear that they are generally higher performing housing managers than local authorities. Within the housing association sector, nevertheless, they set standards which others struggle to match.[4]

By the late 1990s many of the councils that could sell their housing stock for a positive capital value, had made a transfer. Most were district councils, where the majority of dwellings were houses rather than flats, and in reasonable condition. It was becoming clear that transfer would only take place in the major urban areas if the Government offered help with extra funding to bring the existing housing stock to a satisfactory condition.

In 1993 the Joseph Rowntree Foundation published a seminal report *Building Communities*, based on a study of new housing association estates carried out by David Page. The stimulus to the project had come from a growing concern about the management problems being experienced on some of the newly built estates completed by housing associations. The Rowntree report described the major changes in the development programmes of housing associations that had taken place, especially the shift from the renovation of inner city street houses to building purpose built new housing estates.[5]

The Rowntree report received widespread publicity. In the sometimes frenetic debate that followed its publication some associations jumped to over-simplistic conclusions. They saw the cause of the problem as too many homeless families and blamed local authorities for nominating too high a proportion of lettings to new estates. Some commentators went still further. That housing associations were facing the same problems of local authorities was seen as evidence of 'the stigma of social housing'. Their conclusion was that not just council housing, but that social housing as a whole had failed.

The financial advantage of transferring ownership to housing associations was that they could borrow money from private lenders outside Government controls on public spending. In the early phases almost all the transfers were by local authorities where the outstanding debt on the housing stock was low, so that the council benefited from a capital receipt from the sale. While most invested the money in new rented housing, some authorities chose to spend the money on new schools, swimming baths and even civic centres.

In 2002 the Labour Government introduced a new option – the Arm's Length Management Organisation (ALMO) – through which housing management responsibilities would be transferred to the new body, but without a transfer of ownership. It was introduced because the Government recognised there was implacable opposition by some tenants and councils to a transfer of ownership, including some of the authorities with the largest number of dwellings. The ALMO was seen as the only realistic alternative to direct council management.

Because of its poor condition the housing stock owned by some urban authorities had a negative capital value and needed to be transferred with a 'dowry' to make the deal financially viable. Without that those authorities would not be able to comply with the Government's policy that all housing authorities should bring their housing stock up to a satisfactory condition (what the Government has termed the 'decent homes standard') by 2010.

Local authorities that set up an ALMO would receive the capital allocations needed to meet the decent homes standard, but only where they were recognised as performing well. In 2002 the Government set up a Housing Inspectorate in the Audit Commission, with the role of carrying out inspections to assess how well local authority housing departments were providing services. To qualify for ALMO funding they needed to be awarded the top rating of three stars, or at least 'two stars and improving', from the Housing Inspectorate. The extra money was not available to everyone, it was a 'carrot' to reward good performance.

In the first two years 27 councils were given conditional capital allocations of £664 million, towards a total estimated need for capital investment of £1.8 billion. As the average housing stock of these authorities is high, these ALMOs contain 360,000 properties. They include Leeds with almost 70,000 properties, Kirklees with 28,000, Salford with 26,000, Barnsley with 24,000, and Bolton with 21,500. At the time of writing another 15 local authorities have decided that they want to follow the ALMO route, and it is likely that this will rise as more local authorities complete their stock option appraisals.

As any capital expenditure by an ALMO counts as public sector borrowing, there is no difference between spending by an ALMO and spending where the authority retains direct responsibility for its housing stock. There is no objective basis for treating ALMOs differently from directly council run housing departments. The difference results solely from Government policy.

For the past twenty years there has been a widely held belief, including the Conservative and Labour Governments, that local authorities should give up their landlord role, because they were not seen as carrying it out well. The 'Defend Council Housing' lobby, mostly made up of council tenants and trade unionists opposed to stock transfer, had waged a lonely battle against the prevailing consensus. Branding proposals for stock transfer, and more recently ALMOs, as 'privatisation', it has urged tenants to vote 'No' in the ballots.

Most politicians have dismissed the Defend Council Housing Campaign as an unpleasant irritant, which does not represent the views of the majority of tenants. However, there has also been a growing lobby against stock transfer among MPs, led by the fiercely independent Labour MP Austen Mitchell. Although tenants have voted in favour of most transfer proposals, there have been 76 ballots against stock transfer, most importantly in Birmingham, the largest housing authority in England, where almost two-thirds of tenants and leaseholders voted against transfer.

In 2003 a ballot in the London Borough of Camden on plans for an ALMO exposed the arbitrary nature of the Government's policy. If the tenants and leaseholders had voted for an ALMO the council would have received an extra £283 million over the next six years to bring the housing stock up to the decency standard. Because they voted no, by a majority of 70 per cent to 30 per cent, the extra funding was lost, despite the fact that the housing service had been awarded three star status and that the Audit Commission had rated it as the fifth best service in the country, and despite it being in a high-stress inner London area and facing particularly demanding housing management challenges.

At the 2004 Labour Party conference the leadership was defeated on a proposal from the Party's Policy Forum that capital funding should be available to local councils on an equal basis, irrespective of whether tenants had voted for stock transfer, to set up an ALMO or to stay with the local authority. However, subsequent statements by Government Ministers re-asserted the policy that local authorities would not receive extra funding to meet the Decent Homes Standard if they retained direct management responsibility for their housing.

When the Conservative Government introduced plans for stock transfer it was seen as the means of removing housing from the direct control of local authorities. The argument to justify this was that the responsibility for *housing management* should be separated from the *wider strategic housing role* of local authorities. A similar argument has been used in support of ALMOs, even though this does not involve a change of ownership. However, there is no empirical or research *evidence* to justify the view that the separation of housing management responsibility is likely to lead to a better service.

In the late 1980s there was a virtual collapse of the housing service in a number of local authorities, especially some of the inner London boroughs. By contrast, housing associations were seen as being more efficient and more tenant focused. The associations with substantial development programmes were also seen as providing a better 'product' than local authorities.

The position now is very different. There have been steady improvements in the performance of local authorities, both in the management of their own stock and in their wider housing role, including the homelessness services, their role in the private rented sector and the development of comprehensive strategies.

In 2003 the Housing Inspectorate was given the role of inspecting housing associations as well as local authority housing services. The results of the inspections show that the best housing authorities compare well with the best registered social landlords (RSLs), and that they are able to combine successfully their strategic housing role with the effective management of their housing stock.

It has become commonplace for pundits to speak of 'the end of council housing', and a few years ago this looked like a plausible prediction. It now looks a less likely outcome. The ALMO route has offered an attractive option for a growing number of local authorities, and more will follow if it remains a way of gaining extra capital funding. At December 2004 there were just under 150 councils which had not voted on a stock transfer or ALMO option, but it is likely that a significant number will still do so after completing their stock appraisal. However, the fact that they have not done so earlier suggests that there is either significant opposition or a marked lack of enthusiasm to a transfer option. Authorities with low star ratings have been ruled out of being considered for ALMO status. There is no obstacle to pursuing stock transfer other than unwillingness by either the local authority or its tenants, or both.

The impetus for the policy has in almost all cases come from the opportunity that transfer has created for greater capital spending on the housing stock, through the capital receipts from the sale (where these exist) or from being able to borrow money outside the restrictions of the Public Sector Borrowing Requirement. There is little evidence one way or another to show what role the wish to have a new landlord played in these decisions.

There is now the need for a radical re-think of Government policies for providing housing services for tenants and lessees. This should be based on seeking those arrangements that will deliver the best quality, and most cost effective and user-focused services:

- The assessments of what arrangements will deliver this should be based on evidence. They should not be driven by political dogma or untested policy assumptions. The policy should be output driven and evidence based.
- The Government should abandon its presumption that the separation of housing management from the strategic housing role is preferable, until evidence-based assessment has been made of the different options.
- Local authorities that achieve high standards of performance (three star ratings) should be eligible for capital allocations to spend on bringing their housing stock up to the decency standard.

The principle should be that local councils and their tenants are free to make a choice over the ownership and management of their housing, without the options being biased by arbitrary Government rules over access to capital funding.

Chapter 6

Building sustainable communities

The previous chapters have described the changes in tenure that have taken place over the past half-century: the growth of home ownership and the changing nature of rented housing. During the last twenty years there have also been changes in the balance of housing demand and supply, which have reflected growing regional differences.

In the first half of the twentieth century, population growth slowed as families had fewer children. The assumption made in the official planning reports at the end of the war was that the population would remain largely stable. It was projected that new housing would replace the homes destroyed by the war and relieve the acute overcrowding, especially in the congested old cities. This strategy was derailed by the unexpected growth in the post-war population and the trend towards smaller households. The result of this massive demographic change was that the number of separate households almost doubled, from 12 million in 1951 to 22 million in 2001. The growth in the number of households over the past fifty years has been almost as great as that over the whole of the previous 1,000 years!

There have been three main causes for this growth. First, longer life expectancy, combined with the better over-all health, has meant that old people are living longer in their own homes. Second, more people of working age are living alone. This includes people living on their own after divorce or separation, not living with a partner until later in life, or remaining single.

Third, the number of people coming to live in Britain has been greater than the number leaving. While media publicity and public debate has focused most on people arriving in this country as asylum seekers, most of those coming have been economic migrants.

This rapid household growth is not unique to Britain, but has been a common phenomenon among advanced industrialised countries across Europe. What has been different in this country is the extent of the geographically uneven pattern of growth and the failure to match the number of dwellings with the increase in households. In the north the increase in the number of homes has been greater than the growth in the number of households. In the south the opposite has happened, with household growth exceeding housing supply.

One important ingredient in the post-war vision was the belief that the state should play a much stronger role in deciding where industry developed and new homes were built. For over thirty years the controls over the location of industry – and after 1965 on new offices – had some impact on channelling new investment and employment into the least prosperous and peripheral regions, through the granting of industrial development certificates and programmes of regional assistance.

Despite these powers there was uneven regional economic growth, leading to two growing divides: between *north and south* and between the *inner cities* and the *suburbs and market towns*. The loss of employment has been heavily concentrated in the inner cities, where most of the declining industries had been based. Investment and new jobs were attracted to the less congested sites and better environment on the built-up fringes or the towns beyond the green belts. The collapse of the traditional manufacturing, shipbuilding and mining industries led to a massive loss of jobs in many areas of the north. Chapter 10 describes the effect of economic and population decline on one major city, Liverpool.

The problems of low housing demand

As a result, in some areas of the north there are now too few jobs and a surplus of housing. In the last ten years the number of new homes built in the northern regions has exceeded the growth in households. One consequence of this has been a rising concern over low demand for housing – and even abandonment – in some areas, especially in the northern conurbations and in old mining and textile areas.

Initially the issue was raised by managers of social housing, who were seeing higher turnover and vacancy rates and problems in letting housing in some neighbourhoods. The problems were being experienced especially in neighbourhoods where there was a high incidence of crime and problems of anti-social behaviour. Some people attributed the falling demand to the 'stigma of social housing', where people were opting for any alternatives to renting from social landlords.

In 1998 the Social Exclusion Unit (SEU) was commissioned by the Prime Minister to carry out a major study on the problems of the most disadvantaged neighbourhoods, including a Policy Action Team on Unpopular Housing, which was set up to investigate the scale and causes, and recommend necessary action. It was able to draw on the findings of a major research study led by Glen Bramley at Strathclyde University, which included a postal survey of all local authorities and case studies in selected areas. It showed that low demand was extensive in urban areas of the north, and included whole neighbourhoods being abandoned. It identified the key factors, showing that there were specific problems that increased the likelihood of a particular neighbourhood becoming unpopular, but that the underlying causes of low demand for housing were *structural*, that is low levels of employment and an overall surplus of housing.[1]

The research also showed that the worst problems were found in areas of concentrated urban poverty. These include all the measures of deprivation: low levels of employment, high ratios of single parents, poor educational achievement, high incidence of offending and anti-social behaviour and high levels of neighbourhood dissatisfaction.

The problems of failing housing markets in the north and shortages of homes in the south are now recognised as important political issues, but there are sharp differences of opinion about both the causes of the problems and the policy response. Some put the blame for the problems on unfair bias by government against the north and on the failure to restrict growth in the south; some argue that it is not possible to stop the power of market forces and no more can be done to prevent regional inequality; others say the causes are the failure of the house building industry and successive governments to increase housing supply in the south.

At the extremes these views are reflected in polarised policy positions.

Accept the inevitability of decline

The Government cannot reverse the flow of market forces. If we want London to thrive as a leading world city and Britain to compete successfully with other European countries, we must accept that firms want to invest and people to live in the south. The priority for public spending is to make housing affordable and to invest in the infrastructure for new communities.

Let the south stew

The Government should be doing nothing to offset the costs of overpriced housing and congestion in the south, and should rely on market incentives to persuade more firms and industries to locate outside the south. The priority for public spending should be to increase the attractiveness of working and living in the poorer regions, especially the more deprived areas, through investment in transport, economic assistance and housing renewal.

Both these arguments are flawed. It would be incredibly wasteful to demolish sound homes in northern cities in order to build still more in the overheated areas of the south. As well as the financial costs resulting from more unemployment and declining communities, there is a huge social cost of inequality and deprivation.

The experience of the past decade shows that inadequate housing supply does not persuade people to move to other regions. What it has led to is rising prices, more of household incomes spent on housing costs, more forced sharing and more homelessness. Failing to build more homes will not help the north. It will simply increase the problems in the south. Alternative policies need to look at what has happened to housing and employment, and to develop policies that seek to increase territorial justice and create a better balance between people, homes and jobs across all areas of the country.

The housing shortage in the south

The explanation for the worsening housing shortage is straightforward. The number of people needing separate homes has been increasing and the number of homes being built has been falling. Meanwhile, new investment in jobs has been heavily concentrated in the south, especially some of the growth 'hotspots' of the south east.

In the post-war years from 1951 up to 1981 the growth in the dwelling stock nationally exceeded the increase in households, so that the housing shortage reduced. Over the past twenty years, however, the growth in the number of households in southern England has exceeded the number of homes built. Between 1981 and 2001 the number of households increased by 3.7 million, while the number of homes grew by only 3 million, a shortfall of 700,000. In 2001 the number of homes built fell to the lowest level since the war.

By the year 2025 the number of households in England and Wales is projected to rise by a further 3.6 million from

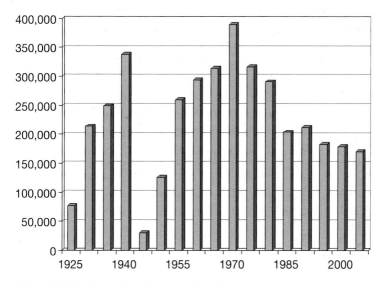

Graph 6.1 Number of new homes built in England

22.2 million to 25.8 million. This is often described as if it is an unprecedented increase, but in fact is no greater than the actual growth over the last twenty years. However, the projected growth in households shows sharp regional differences, with the highest rates in London, the south east, the south west and the east of England, where the housing problems are already most acute. Even with a change towards a redistributive regional economic policy, many more homes will be required in southern England than are currently being built.

Projections on population, household growth and migration have at times been inaccurate in the past, but mostly because they have been too low, not too high. Estimates of the requirement for new homes up to the year 2025 can be revised if experience shows this to be appropriate.

The Communities Plan

In February 2003 the Government published its Communities Plan, a wide-ranging strategy for tackling both the problems of housing shortage and those of low demand. The key elements in the plan are policies for a 'step change in housing supply' in the south, including the Thames Gateway and three new growth areas around Milton Keynes, Stansted and Ashford and to regenerate low demand areas through nine Housing Market Renewal Pathfinder projects in the north and Midlands.

The Government are funding the Pathfinder projects with the remit to draw up strategies that show how successful housing markets can be restored. Chapter 10 includes an account of how this strategy is being implemented through the Housing Market Renewal Initiative in Liverpool.

The concept of 'markets' is central to the approach of all the projects, understanding where and why people move, what prices they will pay and what type of housing they want. This is the basis of decisions on what type of new homes should be built, how existing homes may be modernised, how tenure may be diversified and which dwellings should be demolished,

The issue of demolition is one of the most complex and sensitive. Growing numbers of empty homes are seen as a signal of failure, which prompt people to leave a neighbourhood. This downward spiral can happen with frightening speed. Where the empty homes are obsolescent, demolition is likely to be the best answer, although there may be strong resistance from residents who like their homes and are unwilling to move, especially families who have lived there for many years and worked hard to keep them in good condition.

In other areas the properties may still be in sound condition. The problem is simply that there is an excess of supply, and they are not sufficiently popular with either owners or tenants. The difficult choice is whether it is possible to restore demand through policies of economic regeneration or whether to accept that this is not realistic and to knock down the houses so as to prevent the negative effect of leaving streets of half empty properties.

The widely different character of both housing markets and employment patterns means that the answers are likely to vary between areas. For example, the obstacles to attracting new jobs to the old industrial towns in east Lancashire are very considerable, while the core northern cities are already being successful in securing employment-creating investment.

When the Labour Government established the Regional Development Agencies (RDAs), these were *all* given the remit of seeking to maximise the average level of incomes of people living in their region. Without any positive policy to target explicitly the more deprived areas, new jobs have continued to be created disproportionately in the high-growth regions. In the 2002 Spending Review Statement, Gordon Brown, the Chancellor of the Exchequer, for the first time adopted the policy of seeking to reduce the persistent gap in growth between the regions, and this is included as one of the key Public Service Agreement targets. In his 2003 Budget statement he re-stated this aim, with specific proposals for relocating at least 20,000 public service jobs from London. However, the Government have retained the target that all RDAs should seek to maximise the growth of incomes.

Of course, private companies will not locate their activities where they believe the market opportunities are inferior, but the Government has a wide range of policy tools to influence where jobs are created, including through fiscal policies, programmes of public investment and through their direct control of public agencies. It should also have an explicit policy aim of supporting the location of new publicly supported projects in the less prosperous regions. Manchester's experience in promoting the Commonwealth Games shows how this can be done successfully.

Building sustainable communities

The key challenge is to develop housing policies that learn from past mistakes and set out plans for homes and communities in the twenty-first century. The vision should be to provide sufficient good quality homes for all, where people live in socially balanced neighbourhoods that reflect the diversity of society, and where people in all tenures have choice over where they live. Translating that vision into practice is a huge task, which can only be achieved over a generation.

The report of the Barker Review, quoted in Chapter 2, gives estimates of how many homes are needed in order to increase affordability. The conclusion is that doubling the number of homes built is necessary to meet the shortfall in housing supply, and to reduce the growth in house prices to the average of other European countries. Still more would be needed to achieve the zero house-price inflation that Germany has experienced over the past thirty years.

> Keeping affordability for new households in line with that in the 1980s would imply a current shortfall of between 93,000 and 146,000 homes per annum in England, of which 20,000 to 45,000 are owner occupied private homes and 73,000 to 101,000 are affordable.
>
> Reducing the long-term trend in house prices to zero real growth would imply an *additional* 240,000 homes per annum across the UK. To lower real trend price to 1.1 per cent, 145,000 *more* houses per annum might be needed, about double the current private sector housing output of 150,000 units.[2]

A target of 300,000 homes a year to achieve even the lower number estimated as being required in the Barker Review will be a huge challenge for both house builders, local authorities and housing associations. Yet it is no more than the number built fifty years ago when Harold Macmillan was the Minister for Housing. It is less than the 370,000 built in 1968 when Harold Wilson was the Prime Minister. It is also fewer per head of population than the number of homes being built annually by France, Germany and other countries in the European Union.

Annual house building targets of 300,000 homes a year may immediately evoke images of the mass housing projects of the past. Yet homes need not be developed in large estates, whether private or public, and certainly not in large single tenure estates of rented housing. There should be a diversity of housing types and tenures, including homes for sale, self-built homes, shared ownership, market renting and socially rented, with resident-controlled housing co-operatives and tenant managed homes.

During the last few years there has been strong opposition to proposals for increasing house building in the south east. Serious concerns have been raised over the environmental implications of higher levels of house building, especially the impact of greater traffic use, the effects of higher rates of water use and waste production, and the risks of flooding in low-lying areas, especially around the Thames estuary. In view of these concerns the results of an opinion survey carried out by MORI, reported in the research carried out for the IPPR Commission on Sustainable Development, in the south east are significant.[3] The survey asked a cross-section of residents what issues they thought were a problem. The top issue was the cost of housing (85 per cent) followed closely by traffic levels (82 per cent), and then by housing shortage (58 per cent) and public transport (50 per cent). These were all rated significantly higher than lack of amenities (28 per cent), job availability (28 per cent) and poor quality/lack of parks (21 per cent).

A second survey asked residents in 14 different areas to rate five issues according to their importance. These were affordable housing, public transport, parks and open spaces, low level of traffic and congestion, and low level of pollution. Affordable housing was ranked as the most important in 11 of the areas, and highly in two of the other three. It was rated as the most important in all four areas located within the Government's proposed 'growth areas' in the south east (Milton Keynes in the east Midlands, Medway and Thanet in the Thames Gateway, and Ashford in Kent).

The conclusions that can be drawn from this are very significant. The issues of the cost of housing, housing shortage and the need for affordable housing are consistently seen as the most important issues for residents in the south east, and higher than issues such as availability of employment opportunities and convenient transport which feature highly in national surveys. It is likely that a similar survey of residents in London, which was not covered by the IPPR survey, would show still higher levels of priority to the need for more affordable housing in view of the severity of the problems in London.

What the survey also revealed, however, was the contradictions in people's preferences. While most people recognised the need for more new homes, at the same time a high proportion were opposed to any new homes being built near where they lived themselves. About half of all residents agreed that more housing was needed, with about a third disagreeing. However these proportions were reversed when people were asked their views about more homes being built in their areas, with only a third agreeing that more homes are needed in the area and just over half disagreeing.

The responses are a graphic illustration of the 'nimbyist' views which many people hold, but also evidence that a significant majority of people believe that more homes are needed in the south east. While public authorities must do all that they can to develop plans for new housing which secure as much popular support as possible – by careful planning of location, type of housing, quality of design and other factors – they also have a responsibility not to let their plans be blocked by opponents influenced only by their narrow self-interest.

Table 6.1 Attitudes to new house building

To what extent to you agree or disagree that:	Disagree	Agree	Net agree
More homes are needed in the south east	32%	50%	+18%
More homes are needed in my local area	52%	34%	−18%

The need for more affordable housing

A key ingredient in the Communities Plan is the proposal for more affordable housing, defined as housing for people not able to meet the full market cost. However, despite increases in Government spending the levels of planned investment are significantly lower than independent experts estimate to be needed.

The most recent estimate of the need for affordable housing is in *Building for the Future* by Alan Holmans *et al.*,[4] which updates previous work for Shelter's Housing Investment Project. The conclusion is that there is a need for 67,000 dwellings a year to meet newly arising need each year between 2001 and 2011. In addition an extra 22,000 homes each year are needed to halve the backlog over that period. This gives a total of 89,000 affordable homes annually.

The most significant reason why previous estimates of housing requirements have fallen short of actual need is that they have taken no account of the backlog of existing unmet housing need. The failure to provide for this has been one of the most serious – and inexplicable – omissions in planning policy. The 'backlog' is actually the housing crisis we see around us – the thousands of homeless families spending years in temporary accommodation and the single people with nowhere to stay but on friends' floors or in emergency hostels. Leaving it out of the estimates of need is rather like a hospital ignoring its waiting list and only planning to carry out operations for people who become ill in the future.

For years the Government has issued planning guidance to local authorities on how they plan for the number of homes that are needed. However, this guidance has ignored the need to include the backlog of existing unmet housing need in the assessments, and has only required planning authorities to include newly forming households in their plans.

Encouragingly, the importance of including the backlog is at last being recognised. A crucial breakthrough came with the London Plan, published in February 2004. This includes the backlog in its assessment of overall housing need and endorses the estimate of the backlog of 112,000 households made by the Mayor's Housing Commission. The Government's Communities Plan includes a reference to the backlog in its statement of housing need for London. This is the first time a Government statement has done this, and implies a change of attitude within the Office of the Deputy Prime Minister.

An important question is: what should be the balance between different types of affordable housing? Looking at the assessments of need carried out by local authorities there is a very strong case for the majority of new homes being socially rented homes for people on low incomes, including homeless households in temporary accommodation, families in severely over-crowded homes and vulnerable people needing housing with support. Conversely, a persuasive argument can be made for giving high priority to 'key workers' who are essential to running public services and sustaining a thriving economy.

The broad composition of what is needed nationally each year is 60,000 rented homes and 30,000 for low cost home owner-ship and sub-market rented housing. The balance between different types of housing will differ between areas, and the need for different types of affordable housing should be systematic-ally assessed through local housing strategies.

The estimated cost in public spending for this programme is £7 billion a year. This would require £3.5 million more than the current level of spending on social housing investment.

Delivering the programme for new homes

To meet the target of building more affordable new homes the Government is seeking to achieve substantial savings in the cost of developing social housing, so as to secure greater value from the public spending allocated to the programme. This follows the recommendations of both the Egan report and the Barker Review that the costs of housing production could be significantly reduced.

Greater efficiency is being sought in a number of different ways. A key change is the use of partnering, in place of the traditional adversarial relationship between clients and contractors. The new approach came out of the Government-commissioned Egan report, *Re-thinking Construction* which demonstrated the delays, inefficiencies and extra costs caused by the process of treating every building contract as a one-off operation. The key aims of partnering are to develop long-term relationships between housing associations, developers, building contractors and suppliers based on a shared aim of achieving a high-quality product at the lowest possible cost.

The Housing Corporation is seeking to improve the efficiency of its housing investment by channelling 80 per cent of its development programme for 2004 to 2006 through 70 'partnering' housing associations, chosen on the basis of their overall performance and good development track record. Most smaller associations, including most community-based and black and ethnic minority associations are being encouraged to develop new homes through arrangements with the partnering associations.

Cost reductions are also being sought through greater use of modern methods of construction, especially greater use of off-site assembly. The use of prefabrication of building components is much less common in the UK than in many countries, due in large part to the bad reputation of many industrialised building systems used in the 'mass housing' programme described in Chapter 3. The modern methods are very different from the discredited systems of that era, and experience of new systems shows that there can be significant benefits over traditional site based construction, including lower costs and savings in time taken to build new homes.

One new provision in the 2004 Housing Act is the power for the Housing Corporation to pay social housing grants to organisations other than registered social landlords (RSLs). This has been interpreted as a means of paying grants to private developers, but the powers also could be used to pay grants where the housing is managed by Arm's Length Management Organisations. The Government has allocated £200 million for an initial programme in 2005, and also stated that by 2006/8 the whole of the Housing Corporation's Approved Development Programme should be open to bids from non-RSLs.

It is anticipated that some bids will be made by partnerships between private developers and existing registered social landlords, where the responsibility for building the homes will be with the developer, but the long-term ownership and management will be with the RSL. However bids can also be made where private companies own and manage the properties themselves.

As private developers are not subject to the statutory obligations and systems of regulation that apply to RSLs, the Housing Corporation has announced that separate arrangements will be made for accrediting and monitoring non-RSLs which receive grants. However, there has been widespread criticism that these arrangements will not have equivalent powers of enforcement to those which apply to RSLs and it would be possible for private companies to break the assurances given when the bids for grants were made, without the Housing Corporation having effective sanctions to prevent abuse. As a remedy against this, the Housing Corporation has decided that a 'rent charge' can be made against organisations that breach the terms of the contract, giving the Housing Corporation overriding powers to exert control.

As a result especially of rising land values many local authorities are seeking to secure financial contributions from developers through what are termed Section 106 agreements, referring to the clause in the planning legislation that defines the powers given to local authorities. When granting planning permission for new developments local authorities have powers to make agreement conditional on the applicant providing funding for community benefits. These are now being widely used to require developers to contribute to the cost of providing affordable housing.

The granting of planning permission, especially where this involves a change of use, can significantly increase the profits that can be made for carrying out a development. There is a very strong argument that these 'windfall gains' should be shared by the community rather than going solely to the developer. The difficult judgement for a local authority is how much can reasonably be demanded from a developer through a Section 106 agreement. Many developers argue that local authorities are becoming more and more 'greedy' in demanding higher contributions, and that this is discouraging plans for new housing development. Conversely it is argued that local authority planners, with much less experience of the economics of development than their private sector counterparts, are frequently outwitted in negotiations and achieve less than they could.

One important bargaining counter for local authorities is the use of planning policies to stipulate the percentage of new homes that should be affordable. Where the requirement for a proportion of affordable housing is included in a Section 106 agreement a critical question is how the cost of providing the housing should be funded. The cost may be met in full through a social housing grant paid by the Housing Corporation to a housing association, exactly as would happen if this was a 'stand alone' development without any involvement of a private developer. At the opposite end of the spectrum the Section 106 agreement may stipulate that the cost is met in full by the developer without any input of social housing grant. There are also a range of possibilities between the two extremes, including the payment of a social housing grant for the element of socially rented housing with a requirement on the developer to subsidise the element of shared ownership housing.

Those who argue against the inclusion of high targets for affordable housing frequently imply that the developer is expected to meet the full cost of affordable housing and threaten that such demand will 'kill the goose that lays the golden egg'. In practice such requirements are relatively rare, and usually applied in high demand areas where the value of private homes makes it possible to subsidise in full the element of affordable housing.

Where developers are being required to cross-subsidise affordable housing through Section 106 agreements, they seek to limit the cost. The result can be that standards are reduced or that the affordable homes are built in the least attractive area of the site. There are numerous examples of the rented homes being physically segregated from the private housing, adjacent to busy roads, railway lines, commercial buildings and still worse environmental eyesores. In order to prevent this, the Housing Corporation is now insisting that the affordable housing element is fully integrated within new developments, following mixed community principles.

The Thames Gateway

The largest of the growth areas is the Thames Gateway, stretching out eastwards from London through large stretches of Kent and Essex to the estuary of the river. The key opportunities for development include Thurrock, Barking Riverside, the Royal Docks, Stratford and the Lea Valley in the areas north of the river, and at Greenwich, Dartford and Ebbsfleet, with its Channel Tunnel rail link, south of the river.

As London developed as a major world city the docks played a key role in its foreign trading. Their closure in the 1970s had a dramatic impact on the economy of east London. The London Docklands Development Corporation, set up in 1980 by Michael Heseltine as the Secretary of State for the Environment in Mrs Thatcher's Conservative Government, was hugely successful in attracting new office developments, most spectacularly at Canary Wharf on the Isle of Dogs, but far less so in the wider regeneration of east London.

Traditionally the western parts of London have been more prosperous and this is still true today, with much greater poverty and deprivation in east London than west. The Gateway contains large tracts of contaminated land from earlier industrial use, massive landfill sites, unsightly overhead electricity pylons and old gasworks.

What happens in the Gateway will be a critical test of what the policies in the Communities Plan mean in practice.

It could bring new prosperity to east London and the Thames
estuary by attracting new jobs, high-quality housing and sustainable, mixed tenure communities. Alternatively the developments
could result in isolated communities, living in mediocre quality
homes, with too few opportunities for local employment, excessive levels of commuting, extensive environmental damage and
high levels of social exclusion.

In order to achieve the best potential it is vital that some key
policies are consistently applied. It is essential that the basic
infrastructure is in place from when the first new homes are built,
especially schools, shops and public transport. As an example,
the lack of a firm timetable for the extension of the Docklands
Light Railway is a critical issue for the social sustainability of
the Barking Riverside development.

The new communities must provide a wide range of different
types of housing, with the integration of different tenures. It is
essential to avoid the scenario where new communities consist
predominantly of economically active childless adults in private
housing and benefit-dependent single parent families and older
residents in socially rented housing.

Relatively high densities can contribute to the cohesion of
communities, for example by building most homes within
walking distance of schools, shops and public transport. Homes
should be built at minimum densities of 50 persons per hectare,
but there is scope for significantly higher densities in the London
part of the Gateway.

Finally, it is crucial that new developments are integrated
with policies for the whole Thames Gateway area, including
the existing settlements. For example, in east London there
is considerable scope for providing new housing through
infill developments, building on vacant land and redeveloping
unpopular, poor quality blocks of flats. Such developments
can create opportunities for diversifying tenure on existing
housing estates and also make it possible for existing tenants to
choose if they want to move to different areas. It will be important to avoid the scenario where younger and economically active

households move out to new developments, leaving a still higher proportion of older and non-earning residents in deprived neighbourhoods.

One new development, which provides grounds for optimism, is the Millennium Village in Greenwich Peninsula. This has been carried out by a partnership between Countryside Properties, Taylor Woodrow and English Partnership, which acquired the land. The masterplan was drawn up by the architect Ralph Erskine, with a plan for 1,400 homes in a high quality, mixed tenure, mixed use development. Initially only 20 per cent of the homes were designated to be affordable, but the planned size of the development has been expanded to provide 2,500 homes, with 35 per cent being affordable.

The housing includes a wide range of property types at different densities including apartment flats, live/work units and flats specially designed for people with severe disabilities and family houses built close to the school. The different tenures of socially rented, shared ownership and homes for sale are spread throughout the village, with affordable homes built to the same standard as the private housing.

The developers have been set high targets for minimising the environmental impact, especially energy use and water consumption. A combined heat and power scheme, high levels of insulation and access to natural light, energy and water efficient appliances are achieving these targets. By making walking, cycling and public transport easy and accessible options, car use is being discouraged.

From the early days, residents have been active in developing the life of the community, including setting up a Residents' Association, organising an annual village event and encouraging different ways of volunteering. One important development has been the creation of a resident-owned company that is responsible for providing management services for both socially rented and privately owned housing. Surveys of resident views have shown very high levels of satisfaction, especially on the friendliness of the community and appreciation of physical location near the river.

Achieving good quality

An important initiative by the Government has been the setting up of the CABE, the Commission for Architecture and the Built Environment, which is actively seeking to persuade private developers, house builders and housing associations of the importance of good design and quality.

The need for this was underlined by the results of an audit by CABE of 100 recently completed housing developments: 22 per cent of schemes were judged poor, 61 per cent average and only 17 per cent as good or very good.[5]

In order to encourage good design in affordable housing, CABE is working with a number of housing associations to provide advice on how to achieve high design standards in a variety of contexts and to spread knowledge of their experience. One particular aim of the projects is to show how good design can be effective in countering social exclusion.

One outstanding example of high-quality design of new homes is the development of Beaufort Court in Fulham by the Peabody Trust, which was given a Gold standard award under CABE's Affordable House Building for Life (see photograph on page 86). The judges commented that:

> This development succeeds on almost all fronts. It is beautifully designed, detailed and constructed. There is clearly a strong sense of community, with groups already chatting outside their doors. Houses have a small defensible space at the front and long gardens at the back. Staggering the plan at the rear provides privacy.[6]

The post-war experience shows what has happened when quality has been sacrificed for numbers. Now that once again ambitious targets are being set for the number of new homes to be built, there are serious dangers that history will be repeated. There are pressures on developers and house builders to reduce standards in order to bring down costs for private housing, but homeowners can decide how much they pay. The greatest pressures to reduce standards are on housing associations, where future tenants have no say if quality and standards are cut.

Beaufort Court, Lillie Road, Fulham
Peabody Trust

The tougher financial targets being set for housing associations are intended to achieve tighter cost control and efficiency savings, with more homes being built from the budget available. The disadvantage may be that more new homes are built in less attractive neighbourhoods and with the elimination of what are deemed to be non-essential features, even though they would have enhanced the quality of the new homes and their environment.

Both the Government and the Housing Corporation have endorsed the importance of building good quality homes as well as achieving the targets for increasing the number of new homes built. However, the aim will only be achieved in practice if there is a single-minded determination to meet the objectives of both quantity and quality. Housing associations will need to demonstrate that both goals can be met. Residents must be given the opportunity to give their feedback on their experience of living in newly built homes. The Housing Corporation will need to recognise and reward good performance in design and sustainability in deciding on future investment allocations.

This chapter has set out wide-ranging proposals for providing many more good quality new homes. Chapters 8 and 9 put forward proposals for promoting more socially balanced, mixed tenure neighbourhoods and for increasing choice, especially for tenants who cannot afford to buy. Achieving aims need not be a utopian dream but can become practical reality. We need to learn lessons from the past and set out ambitious goals for what is needed.

The greatest obstacle is likely to be lack of money to carry out the programme. Firm estimates are needed on what implementing the policies will cost, and a strong case mounted for the resources needed. The financial costs will be high but so will the benefits, not only in better housing but also in better health, less inequality and greater social cohesion.

What is often forgotten is that current levels of spending are far lower than they were throughout the post-war years until the cuts imposed by the International Monetary Fund in the financial crisis of 1976, which were then followed by the cuts made by the Conservative Government. At constant prices, investment has reduced from £8.3 million in 1980/81 to £3.6 million in 2003/4. Although the Labour Government has increased spending over the past five years, in real terms it is still below the levels of the early 1990s, less than half the level of the 1970s and a third of the level of the 1960s.

Implementing the policies advocated in this chapter is likely to cost £7 billion a year, £3.5 billion more than the current level of spending. With the Government's strict controls on public expenditure this may seem wildly unrealistic, but nothing is gained by pretending the scale of the task is less than it is. There is too much experience of successive governments claiming that their new programmes will solve the housing problems, when in reality they fall far short of what is needed. Underestimating what needs to be done, including how much it will cost, simply leads to disillusionment.

Chapter 13 proposes a new strategy that could provide the increased resources to fund the proposals. If this is not done through the current sources of funding public spending on housing, new sources should be found. It makes the case for taxing the huge untaxed windfall capital gains of homeowners, so as to fund a major increase in investment in good quality affordable homes. These policies also have the advantage of stemming the escalation of house prices and therefore making it more affordable for first time buyers to purchase a home.

Chapter 7

Putting an end to homelessness

Shortly after the 1977 Homeless Persons Act came into force, there were just under 5,000 homeless households in temporary accommodation in England. During the 1980s the number grew rapidly, and by 1990 there were over 45,000 households in temporary accommodation. During the early 1990s the number grew to a peak of 63,000, but then fell to 44,000 in 1996. Since 1997, however, there has been a dramatic rise, with 72,000 households in temporary accommodation in 2000 and over 100,000 households in temporary accommodation in 2004.

The most unsatisfactory form of temporary accommodation is bed and breakfast (B&B 'hotels'). Local authorities have used B&B accommodation for homeless families since the early 1970s. In 1974 Shelter published a hard-hitting report describing the growing use of B&B by some local authorities, and documented the appalling conditions experienced by some families. As a result of campaigning, many local authorities resolved not to use B&B unless there was no alternative. In the Code of Guidance published by the Government when the Homeless Persons Act became law in 1978, local authorities were urged only to use B&B as a last resort.

Regrettably, when homelessness increased during the 1980s the use of B&B grew dramatically, especially in London. There was a public outcry as a result of fires in B&B hotels, including a tragedy in Marylebone where a mother and two young children died. Angry homeless families occupied the Council Chamber in Camden Town Hall and refused to move until

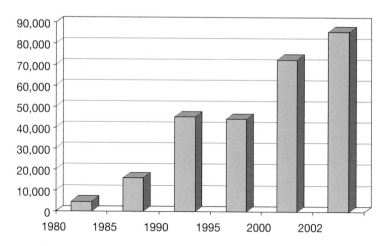

Graph 7.1 Homeless households in temporary accommodation

assurances were given that the council would not in future place homeless families in dangerous B&B hotels. At the inquest the Coroner concluded that the deaths could have been avoided if there had been adequate fire precautions and means of escape.

Despite the risks for families living in B&B, the numbers of homeless families living in them continued to rise until a peak of over 12,000 homeless families was reached in 1991. The numbers then fell, mainly as a result of local authorities using accommodation leased from private owners. Most councils used housing associations to procure and manage this accommodation. The conditions in leased accommodation were almost always much better; families had self-contained accommodation, without having to share kitchens, bathrooms and toilets as they did in B&B. Despite paying market rents to the landlords, the costs of leasing were significantly lower than those of B&B. For the homeless families and the local councils it was a win-win. The accommodation was not only better: it was also cheaper.

By 1994 the numbers of homeless families in B&B had fallen to almost 4,000. Local authorities in London had developed joint arrangements for inspecting and monitoring B&B hotels, grading them according to their conditions. Councils refused to place families in any hotels that failed to comply with the minimum standards. Even if the hotels were still expensive, at least they were safe.

Regrettably the lower use of B&B was short-lived, and the numbers began to grow again. In 2001 the Government announced a target for all local authorities to end the use of B&B for homeless families, (although not for single people) by April 2004. In order to achieve this target a Bed and Breakfast Unit was set up, and a special fund was set up to help local authorities provide alternatives to B&B. As a result of a concerted effort, the number of homeless families in B&B was cut to fewer than 1,700 by December 2003, a reduction of two thirds, although there were still over 6,500 single people or couples without children.

The quality of temporary accommodation used by local authorities is mostly far better than it was in the 1970s and 1980s, especially where properties are leased from private owners. The problem is that it is *costly* and it is *temporary*.

In London, families in leased accommodation typically have to pay weekly rents of £300 a week or more. They are able to claim housing benefit, but where someone is in a low paid job almost all their wages can be taken up by the rent. As a result tenants are no better off working than relying on income support. When costs of travel, meals and childcare are included they may be worse-off working than staying at home. They are caught in the poverty trap, with no incentive to get a job, except in the 'informal' economy.

For homeless families the worst aspect of temporary accommodation is the lack of stability. In London, families may spend two or three years, and some even longer, in temporary accommodation. Quite often families have to leave one property because the lease has expired, and move to another temporary home. Children often have to move schools several times, with inevitable disruption to their education.

Becoming homeless is a traumatic experience. The difficulties are especially severe for those such as families who have lost their home as a result of domestic violence, or refugees who have both lost their home and been forced to escape from their own country. The combination of personal stress and changing schools can mean that children experience such disruption to their education that they never catch up.

An Emergency Homelessness Programme

Yet there is a straightforward solution. In London it would be possible to *end* the use of temporary accommodation for homeless families and single people *within five years*. In all but a few other areas of the country it could be done in two years, and in most cases without the need for any increase in public spending.

The only exceptions would be where temporary accommodation is provided to vulnerable people while an assessment is made of the kind of accommodation that is needed, or in providing accommodation with intensive support to help them prepare for living independently.

What the Government should do is launch an Emergency Homelessness Programme for buying properties on the open market, doing any necessary repairs or conversions, and letting them to homeless families living in temporary accommodation. The properties could be bought directly by local authorities or by housing associations that would make them available to local authorities.

Currently local authorities are paying market rents to lease properties from private owners to provide temporary accommodation for homeless families. Most residents depend on housing benefit to pay the rent, so the cost in public spending is high. Families in temporary accommodation do not have the stability of a settled home. Children frequently have to change schools, or face long journeys if they stay at the school they went to before the family became homeless. It would be far better for the homeless families and no more expensive for the local authorities to buy the leased properties and let them on long-term tenancies.

As a result of high house prices the cost of purchasing properties would be high, probably £150,000 per unit, assuming larger properties were converted into two or more flats. So the estimated capital cost of providing accommodation for 20,000 homeless households a year would be £3 billion.

However, there would be substantial savings on housing benefit, as the rents on normal council and housing associations tenancies are far lower than the rents in leased accommodation.

The properties bought would be similar to those being leased from private owners. These are mostly individual street properties, not flats on housing estates. In some instances it would be possible to buy property directly from the owner who is leasing it as temporary accommodation. Some families could stay where they are and become secure council tenants, without any need to move again.

In the most expensive areas, and those areas with fewer street properties, it would not be possible to buy enough properties within the borough. However, not all homeless families want homes in the borough where they became homeless, and some are already living in temporary accommodation outside the borough.

This idea may seem impracticable, but something similar has happened before, although for different reasons. In 1993 the Conservative Government announced a 'Housing Market Package'. The housing market had collapsed and private house builders owned thousands of properties that they were unable to sell. In response to their cries of anguish the Government launched a special 'housing market programme', which provided funding for housing associations to buy unsold properties from builders in order to let them as tenanted homes.

There were a number of difficulties with the programme, mainly because the housing had not been designed and built for such a high proportion of families with young children, but for owner-occupiers who were mainly single people or couples without children. However, these problems do not invalidate the aim of the policy. The Housing Market Package showed that housing associations could purchase a large number of properties from private owners in a short period of time, and let them to tenants in housing need. If it was right to do it to help private house builders with a cash flow crisis surely it must be much more desirable to do it for homeless families to avoid them having to spend years in temporary accommodation.

Even more relevantly, the argument for converting temporary accommodation into permanent homes was put in the report of the Prime Minister's Strategy Unit *London Project Report*, published in July 2004, which said 'Expenditure on temporary accommodation should be converted to construction or purchase of permanent homes.'

In those areas of the country where the shortage of housing is less severe a different solution is possible. There is a widespread belief that most new lettings by councils and housing associations go to families who have become homeless. In fact only 33 per cent of council lettings and 20 per cent of housing associations lettings in 2003/4 went to households who had been accepted as homeless by a local authority.

Simply by increasing the percentage to 50 per cent for a limited period the number of homeless households could be reduced quickly. Of course this would mean giving lower priority to another group, such as applicants on the housing waiting list. However, this policy would only be needed for a limited period. The choice is simple. It is undesirable that homeless families should have to go through all the trauma of becoming homeless and having to live in temporary accommodation before being given a permanent home. Avoiding this should be treated as a high priority by all local authorities, even when this means that some other applicants with less housing need have to wait longer.

On these assumptions the Emergency Homelessness Programme would be needed for five years. After this period what is needed is to ensure that the flow of lettings into permanent homes matches the acceptance of homeless households. Each local authority should agree a Target Allocation Policy each year; make a realistic estimate of the number of homeless households; calculate the number of new lettings that will be available – from existing tenants moving and from new accommodation – and then decide what percentage of those new lettings will be needed to re-house those who have been accepted as homeless. Provided the lettings match the re-housing of homeless applicants there will be no need for temporary accommodation.

Over the past twenty-five years the use of temporary accommodation has become accepted as normal, even inevitable. Yet it is not necessary, and deeply damaging. When people become homeless what they need is to move to a stable home as soon as possible. Moving home is a stressful process for everyone, even those who move home by choice. Requiring people who have lost their homes to endure repeated moves is inhumane.

Homeless single people

This growth in the use of temporary accommodation is shocking, but the full scale of homelessness is still greater. The official statistics record only the households accepted as homeless by local authorities. They have a legal duty to provide accommodation for households who are in 'priority need', which includes families with dependent children and women expecting a child, but only those single people who are assessed as 'vulnerable', because of mental or physical illness or disability, as a result of living in an institution or because of their age.

All other single people who become homeless are only entitled to 'advice and assistance', which often amounts to no more than offering a list of private letting agents or cheap bed and breakfast hotels. As a result most homeless single people have to fend for themselves. Many end up sleeping on the floors or sofas of friends. Others stay in hostels or emergency night shelters. For those who can find nowhere at all to stay the only option is to sleep on the street. 'Sleeping rough' is the most extreme and visible form of homelessness. When many people talk about homelessness, this is what they mean, yet it is only the tip of the iceberg. So the official homeless statistics exclude most single people.

The real problem of homelessness is experienced by those people who have little chance of finding a permanent home, many of whom have difficulties caused by mental or physical ill-health or substance misuse. Everyone has their own individual story, but there are some experiences that greatly increase the risks of becoming homeless. These include young people who have been in care or 'looked after' as a child, people who have lived in institutions (whether psychiatric hospital, prison or the armed forces) or people who have lost their home as a result of a breakdown in a relationship.

Homeless people who are 'vulnerable' are entitled to be accepted as in 'priority need' if they apply to local authorities. Approximately a third of all households accepted as homeless are single people. In the past they have frequently been offered a one bedroom unfurnished flat and expected to cope, without being offered any extra support. However, many of the most vulnerable homeless people do not apply to local authorities because they believe that they are not able to cope with a flat on their own.

Until the 1980s many homeless single people lived in large institutional hostels. Some were run by commercial landlords, including the huge Rowton hostels in London; some by voluntary organisations or churches, especially the Salvation Army and Church Army; some by local authorities, including Liverpool and Manchester and some inner London boroughs; and the Government-run Reception Centres.

The conditions in many of these hostels were primitive. Residents slept in communal dormitories or tiny single rooms. Bathrooms and toilets were shared by large numbers of people. The regimes were typically authoritarian, and at worst brutal.

One notorious example was Bruce House, an old-fashioned common lodging house, run by Westminster City Council in London. Most residents had to sleep in tiny cubicles measuring seven feet by four feet. There were only five baths and one shower for 695 residents. A public health inspector's report 1980 identified 236 defects, many of which were health and safety risks.

In 1981 a BBC TV reporter, Tony Wilkinson, made a film inside Bruce House, unknown to the management, and wrote a book, *Down and Out*, that described what he found. Among many shocking discoveries he found that the fire doors were locked, despite earlier claims by the local authority that this practice had been stopped. He wrote 'I could not comprehend the minds of men who risked other people's lives for their administrative convenience'.

In the 1960s a handful of new voluntary organisations were created because their founders believed that the traditional agencies were failing to reach the most vulnerable homeless people. Anton Wallich Clifford started the Simon Community, opening communal houses for homeless people however destitute; Jim Horne founded St Mungo's, a hostel in a former Marmite factory in south London; and an Anglican priest, Revd Kenneth Leech, started Centrepoint in Soho, central London, offering a night centre for homeless young people.

With little or no help from statutory funding, these agencies operated on a shoestring. They were run by highly committed, but poorly paid staff, who were often helped by dedicated volunteers. Among the founders were some inspirational and charismatic leaders, as well as one or two rogues. Most had no previous experience of running organisations, and the style of management ranged from autocratic to chaotic.

In the 1970s the Government started to accept greater responsibility for supporting services to homeless single people, spurred by pressure from the 'Campaign for the Homeless and Rootless' (CHAR), several powerful TV documentaries and growing public concern. A number of voluntary agencies were set up in London as a result of the Department of Health and Social Security report on the needs of homeless young people, including the Piccadilly Advice Centre.

The homelessness legislation

The 1977 Homeless Persons Act was a groundbreaking piece of legislation. It was the first legislation in any country in the world to place a legal duty on local authorities to secure permanent accommodation for homeless people.

Under the 1948 National Assistance Act the welfare departments of local authorities were required to provide temporary shelter for people in urgent need. The accommodation for families had typically been in emergency hostels, often admitting only women and their children, with residents forced to share bathrooms, toilets and cooking facilities. Not surprisingly, homeless families applied only as the very last resort, when every other attempt to find even temporary shelter had failed. The accommodation for homeless single people was in government-run reception centres, such as the notorious Camberwell 'spike', where applicants had to strip off all their clothing and have a bath before they were admitted.

In 1974 a Government Circular was issued advising that local housing authorities, not their social service departments, should have responsibility for homelessness. However, this advice had no statutory force. The more progressive local authorities accepted the recommendations to provide long-term permanent housing for homeless applicants, but reactionary councils did not. Several thousand children a year were being taken into care because their families were homeless.

The 1977 Homeless Persons Act radically extended the homeless provisions of the National Assistance Act, by placing a legal duty on housing authorities to provide permanent accommodation. The crucial distinction made in the Act was between those applicants which should be treated as in 'priority need' – families with dependent children, women expecting a child and vulnerable single people – and all other single people and couples without a child.

In practice, the provision of the Act was not applied consistently. Local authorities accepted the duty to homeless families, although there have been innumerable disputes over whether applicants were actually homeless, whether they had made themselves 'intentionally homeless', and which council should take responsibility where people had moved from one area to another.

The Code of Guidance issued with the Act provided detailed advice on how the Act should be interpreted and contentious provisions have been clarified by judicial case law. While most local authorities accepted the spirit as well as the letter of the law, a minority persisted in complying only with the legal minimum. Independent voluntary agencies, especially Shelter and law centres, have played a vital role in advising and supporting homeless applicants who have been denied their legal rights.

By contrast, many local authorities have failed to comply with their duties to vulnerable single people. A third of all households accepted as homeless by local authorities are single people deemed to be vulnerable, but in most instances these are people who are able to cope with an independent tenancy, usually without any support. Many local authorities have failed to develop any special provision for single people with addictions, or young people who are not ready to cope with their own tenancy.

Surprisingly, successive governments have done nothing to challenge the behaviour of local authorities. In practice they have acquiesced in their failure, and instead supported the development of alternative forms of specialist provision by voluntary agencies. Local authorities have developed their own role as partners, but outside the framework of the homelessness legislation.

A key initiative was the programme for the replacement of the old institutional hostels and the Government reception centres which began in the late 1970s. Almost all the old hostels were closed. In their place a range of small direct access hostels and supported housing projects have been developed. Residents wanting to move to their own flats have been helped to 'resettle'.

Over the past twenty-five years a complex network of housing and supportive services has been built up for vulnerable single people. Most of the accommodation has been provided by housing associations, with capital grants from the Housing Corporation. The housing has been managed by voluntary agencies, with revenue funding provided through grants from local authorities and central government. The type of accommodation ranges from small hostels with low levels of support to highly staffed hostels for people with intensive needs for care and support, such as people with serious learning disabilities or mental health problems.

The most visible and extreme form of homelessness is living on the street. There have been destitute people without any kind of fixed abode over many centuries, and writers have graphically described their encounters with them. More people were known to be living on the streets in London, but there were others in every large city, as well as in some towns and rural communities.

In the years following the Second World War, however, the number of people sleeping on the streets was small. Numbers grew in the 1960s, and charities such as the Simon Community, the Cyrenians and St Mungo's were set up to provide shelters for homeless people with no fixed abode. In 1970 a count of homeless people on the streets recorded 300 people in London.

In the late 1980s the number of homeless people on the streets in London started to grow sharply. Unlike most forms of homelessness, street sleeping is very visible, and the rising numbers became an issue for the media and politicians, as well as public concern.

In 1990 the Government launched a 'Rough Sleepers Initiative' (RSI), providing funding for voluntary homeless agencies to open direct access hostels and for housing associations to provide 'move on' accommodation for people who had been living on the streets. Regular counts were made every six months to record the number of rough sleepers, covering all the sites where people were known to be sleeping in the open. In 1995 the Government extended the RSI to places outside London, where there were known to be significant numbers of rough sleepers.

Despite these efforts to tackle the problem, however, there was little reduction in the numbers. In 1997 the new Labour Government made the issue of rough sleeping the first remit of its newly created Social Exclusion Unit. Their report set out ambitious proposals for reducing the number of 2,000 rough sleepers by two-thirds over three years. A Rough Sleepers Unit (RSU) was set up within the Department of Environment, Transport and Regional Affairs (DETR), headed by Louise Casey, previously Deputy Director of Shelter. The RSU was allocated £200 million a year of capital and revenue funding.

The Unit developed a highly focused strategy for achieving the targets, commissioning voluntary agencies to make contact with people on the streets, providing temporary housing and support in settling in long-term accommodation. The Housing Corporation funded housing associations to acquire the 'move on' accommodation. The local authorities in the areas with significant numbers of rough sleepers were expected to produce local strategies.

Louise Casey gave the RSU a very visible, and sometimes controversial, profile, with criticisms being made that coercive pressure was being put on people to leave the streets. The agencies participating in the programme were given demanding performance targets, and regular street counts were carried out to measure progress. The target of reducing the number of people sleeping rough was met, six months ahead of schedule, in December 2002.

The research carried out by the Rough Sleepers Unit showed how many people suffered from serious problems of mental illness and addiction to drugs or alcohol. Many had lived in institutions, including prison, hospital or local authority care. Almost all should have been accepted as vulnerable if they had applied to the local authority as homeless.

In practice most rough sleepers had never approached their local council. The Homeless Persons Units of local councils were seen as a route to a council flat. Correctly in most cases they were not seen as equipped to help people with multiple problems sleeping on the street.

A few local authorities had developed special arrangements for helping vulnerable single people who applied as homeless. In the main they welcomed the Government's rough sleeping strategy, especially the extra resources being provided. Services to street homeless people were developed in parallel to those provided under the homelessness legislation.

A new strategy for homelessness

The 1996 Housing Act amended the homelessness duties of local authorities, most importantly by requiring local authorities only to provide temporary accommodation for 24 months to homeless households in priority need. Proposals for changing the homelessness laws were first outlined in the Green Paper in 1994, and were strongly opposed by both voluntary agencies and local authorities. Although the Government went ahead with new legislation, the changes were much less drastic than originally proposed.

The Labour Party included a promise to restore the rights of homeless families to permanent accommodation in its manifesto for the 1997 General Election. It was actually five years before this 2002 Homelessness Act honoured that manifesto commitment, but when it eventually came its provisions went way beyond simply reversing the changes of the 1996 Housing Act.

To the surprise of many housing professionals the Act extended the priority need groups to include all homeless 16 and 17 year olds and anyone under 21 who had been in care, anyone made homeless as a result of violence, and anyone who was homeless on leaving prison, hospital or the armed forces if they were considered vulnerable.

The Act also required all local authorities to draw up a homelessness strategy within 12 months of the Act becoming law. The strategy was to be drawn up in consultation with social services and health authorities. It was specifically required to include policies for preventing homelessness and ensuring that people who became homeless did not become homeless again. Local authorities were encouraged to include voluntary agencies in the development of their homelessness strategies, but could only include the services provided by voluntary agencies in the strategy with their consent.

Not surprisingly some people viewed the duty to draw up yet another strategy with scepticism. There are depressing examples of local authorities and other public agencies producing grand-sounding strategies that yielded little practical change, and the documents soon lay gathering dust. However, experience so far suggests that reaction would be too pessimistic.

The Government's Homelessness Directorate published a research report that provided comprehensive proposals for developing a homelessness strategy. Shelter appointed 30 locally based campaign staff to work with local authorities and voluntary agencies in preparing the new strategies, and the report evaluating this initiative records positive outcomes in many areas.

Few local authorities, however, have recognised the potential for transforming the traditional response to homelessness. The 1977 Homeless Persons Act marked a critically important advance, by placing a legal duty on local authorities to provide accommodation. Yet essentially the Act created a safety net, giving help only when the crisis of becoming homeless was imminent or had already happened.

What the new homelessness strategies should be doing is setting up a network of early warnings. By responding to these, action should be taken that would prevent people becoming homeless. This may sound impractically optimistic. It can be realistic, given the will to think radically and imaginatively about how it can be achieved.

What could be done is best shown by practical examples. It is well established that prisoners face a high risk of becoming homeless when they are discharged from custody. There are already excellent examples of housing advice services in prisons that help in finding accommodation, including links with local councils and other housing providers. The aim should be to ensure that accommodation is available for anyone leaving a prison or young offenders institution, before the day that they leave. Nobody should become homeless on leaving, or need to apply as homeless and spend time in temporary accommodation.

The same approach should be followed with people with mental health problems who have been in residential care. Where patients have been kept compulsorily in hospital, they can only leave when the order detaining them has been lifted. Arrangements should be set up before the patients are discharged, ensuring that not only is appropriate accommodation available, but that whatever support and care may be needed will also be provided.

Across the country womens' refuges give shelter to women escaping domestic violence. They provide desperately needed emergency help to women and their children who are no longer able to stay in safety at their own home. Yet most women only come to a refuge after having experienced repeated incidents of violence. The first violent incident usually only happens after previous threats of violence.

Some domestic violence projects are now encouraging women to seek help before they experience violence, or before repeated incidents have happened. Outreach workers visit women to discuss how they avoid violent attacks. If a transfer to a different home is essential, the aim should be to arrange this before a crisis which forces the women to escape from a violent attack.

gap between council tenant and owner-occupier. Many of the houses originally acquired in the early 1960s with a view to demolition are now being done up and re-let to council tenants, which pleases both the prospective tenants and middle-class conservationists.[6]

When the Notting Hill Housing Trust began it was simply buying properties to house desperately overcrowded families, with no conscious aim of promoting socially balanced, mixed tenure communities. However, as the number of homes owned by the Trust grew, the mix of tenures became an important feature of the neighbourhoods where the Trust was active.

Compared to the single tenure council-owned housing estates, what was different about those neighbourhoods was the way in which owner-occupied, privately rented and housing association properties quietly co-existed in almost every street, usually without being visible to a stranger's eye, let alone commented upon. In an age of growing social polarisation this in itself was a substantial achievement.

Despite the growth of middle class gentrification, much of north Kensington today is a mixed tenure, multi-racial and socially balanced community. Sadly the escalating house prices of the last decade have stopped housing associations buying more properties and now only the very rich can afford to buy properties for sale, and the area is becoming polarised. Yet the poor have not been driven out to make a one tenure enclave of the affluent as seemed likely forty years ago.

North Islington in the late 1960s was one of the worst areas of housing stress in the whole of England. Some housing was being redeveloped to build new council housing estates, but leaving most private tenants living in poorly equipped, multi-occupied and insecure housing. The North Islington Housing Rights Project led a campaign to persuade the council not to clear these properties but to buy them so they could be renovated for the benefit of the existing residents.

In one group of streets in north Islington – the Landseer and Alexander Road area – the council served compulsory purchase notices on all the houses where the landlords failed to comply with an ultimatum to carry out the improvements needed, and after a public inquiry 170 properties out of 360 in the area were acquired by the council so that the houses could be rehabilitated. A small square was made into an open park with public access, trees were planted down each street, all the properties were modernised, and today homeowners and tenants live side by side, with nothing to distinguish the different forms of tenure.[7]

At the same time the Holloway Tenant Co-operative (HTC) opened its office in the area. Its multi-racial membership comprised tenants living in privately owned properties in the area, mostly living in insecure furnished lettings. The co-op bought vacant properties and renovated them for members in the greatest need. Today it has over 500 tenants across four wards of north Islington. Books have been published to record its history, and its work has been discussed in national social policy debate. Yet HTC is invisible. None of its properties can be distinguished from the one next door. They simply fit into the diversity of tenure in every street.

The development of housing for people with special needs provides another example of integrating social housing within areas of predominantly private housing. Since the 1970s housing associations have developed a wide range of small-scale projects, many in partnership with voluntary agencies, for people who need different forms of supported housing. These include accommodation for people with mental health difficulties and learning disabilities, womens' refuges and homes for ex-offenders and vulnerable young people.

While some of these projects are located within social housing estates, most have been developed elsewhere. This policy has avoided housing still more vulnerable people in estates with already high levels of deprivation. While there has been hostility from some neighbouring residents, and local businesses, most of these projects are successfully well integrated within socially diverse communities.

Because most of these projects are not visibly distinct, the scale of this provision is often not recognised. The experience of one leading homelessness agency illustrates the extent of what exists. St Mungo's has 47 different projects, spread across a number of different London boroughs. These include a small number of large hostels, but most of the provision is in supported housing projects, located in ordinary street properties.[8]

In the US the Hope VI project has been successful over the last ten years in promoting the development of mixed income communities through grants to 166 cities, including some of the most troubled cities in the country.

A report, *Mixed Communities in England* by Alan Berube from the Brookings Institute, written while he was on second-ment to HM Treasury in the autumn of 2004, suggests how lessons from the Hope VI projects might be translated into new policies for developing socially mixed communities in this country.

Initially, the Hope VI project focused on redeveloping inner city high-rise public housing projects into lower density, higher quality projects occupied by more economically active families. As it evolved, however, the central premise changed to reflect a new policy ethos in the US:

> Public housing should 'de-concentrate' poverty by helping families to relocate to better neighbourhoods, and should create truly mixed communities in place of distressed developments. . . . If mixed communities are to be an effective response to growing economic segregation, they must represent a policy objective across the full range of places. Such a comprehensive approach would advance the notion that no community should be the exclusive province of either the rich or the poor.[9]

Applying this would require a range of new policies in this country, including that social landlords should acquire or build properties for rent in more settled, middle income communities and fund this by selling properties on low-income estates.

Developing a strategic policy

The goal of 'well integrated mix of decent homes' will not be achieved if it is limited to new housing developments. It will require a far-reaching re-configuration of the pattern of housing tenure, diversifying ownership on single tenure social housing estates and enabling social landlords to acquire homes to rent in neighbourhoods of predominantly private housing.

The strategic aim should be to promote more socially mixed communities across all types of housing. This will reduce the concentration of low-income households in the poorest neighbourhoods, and it will reduce the proportion of social housing tenants living in the least popular flats.

Chapter 7 has set out proposals for an Emergency Homelessness Programme to buy housing for families living in temporary accommodation. These policies would increase the supply of socially rented housing in mixed tenure neighbourhoods. Chapter 9 will outline proposals for enabling tenants to have greater choice, especially through choosing a home available on the private market, where this can be bought for no more than the market value of their existing accommodation. So far as possible existing tenants should be able to choose where they want to live, within reasonable price limits. This policy must not be confined to inner urban areas, but across suburbs, freestanding towns and rural communities.

It will be difficult to implement ambitious proposals for developing socially mixed communities within the current arrangements of social housing. Local authorities' activities are restricted by their geographical boundaries. Registered social landlords now comprise a diverse range of stock transfer properties and homes from past development programmes. Neither have the structures or the powers to spearhead the huge programme of purchase and sales that will be needed.

To enable this programme to happen the Government should give the new Regional Housing Boards powers to oversee it. The Boards would be responsible for the overall strategy and the local authorities would develop their own sub-regional and local housing strategies within this framework. These arrangements would also match well with the proposals for strengthening the role of regional economic and planning policies and integrating these with housing policies.

The form which social housing has taken in Britain was not inevitable and nor is it immutable. It would be possible for local authorities to change radically the portfolio of properties they own, if they believe this is desirable in order to reduce the stark inequalities that have developed, and to respond better to the aspirations of their tenants. Equally, it would be possible to change the pattern of tenure across cities, so as to increase the share of socially rented housing in outer, suburban areas and to reduce it in the inner areas.

Chapter 9

Widening choice

The aims of increasing choice should be to give individual housing applicants and existing tenants of social landlords a greater say in where they live, and wider options on who owns and manages their homes. This chapter will show that there are ways of widening choice without increasing inequality.

The issue of choice in public services has become a key issue in public debate. The Conservative Party promote themselves as the leading protagonists of choice, with proposals that give parents more say over choice of schools for their children and patients more say in where they go for treatment. Their ideas for increasing choice in housing, however, only offer greater choice for people who want to buy. They have no proposals to increase choice for people wanting to rent.

Within the Labour Party the modernisers see increasing choice for users of public services as a key idea across a wide agenda, ranging from the new freedoms given to foundation hospitals to the growth of specialist secondary schools. The traditionalists argue that greater choice is not a priority for users of public services. What people see as most important is having good doctors and hospitals in their local areas, without long waiting times for treatment, and neighbourhood schools where children can receive a good education.

What this debate almost always ignores is the question of choice over where people live. Almost every night now there are TV programmes such as *Location, Location, Location* showing prospective buyers searching for a new home, or *Changing Rooms* filming people doing a 'makeover' of a property they have bought. They are seen as having great popular appeal, identifying with people's aspirations to have the most attractive home possible.

But where are the opportunities for those who do not have budgets of £500,000, £250,000, even £100,000, to purchase their dream house or flat? What happens to all the tenants who cannot afford to buy at all? The programmes are presented as if they have universal appeal yet they totally exclude the least affluent quarter of the population.

Differences in choice have been one of the greatest causes of inequality between homeowners and tenants. While homeowners are able to choose where they live, within the limits of what they can afford, social landlords have traditionally decided what homes prospective tenants are offered. The language itself tells the story. Homes are allocated by the landlord, not chosen by the tenant.

The experience of people seeking accommodation from a social landlord has been made still more unsatisfactory by the paternalistic way in which many of them have managed their allocations. The word itself has indicated that it is the landlords who decided, not the applicant. Most social landlords have made little effort to find out what applicants would prefer. There has been a widespread attitude that tenants should be grateful for what they get. There has also been evidence of racially discriminatory practices, resulting in black and minority ethnic households getting the worst accommodation.

The Commission for Architecture and the Built Environment (CABE) published the results in 2002 of a MORI poll that asked over 1,000 people where they would most like to live from a selection of images of houses. The two most desirable housing types were the bungalow (30 per cent) and the village house (29 per cent), followed by the Victorian terrace (16 per cent) and the modern semi (14 per cent). Nobody put a tower block as their first choice and it was overwhelmingly the type of housing where people least wanted to live.[1]

Those who can afford to buy have a wide degree of choice. In contrast, lower income households seeking social rented accommodation have very limited choice. The lack of choice for people seeking to obtain socially rented housing, or transfers within it, has been limited by bureaucratic rules and an attitude of state paternalism, but also because choices have been limited to the housing stock currently owned by the landlord.

Choice does matter to tenants, just as it matters to home-owners. The challenge is to find ways of enabling tenants to have greater choice, without also increasing inequality, even if inadvertently.

Over recent years considerable progress has been made by both local authorities and housing associations in increasing the degree of choice which applicants have over offers of accommodation. In 2000 the Housing Minister, Nick Raynsford, made a decision in the Housing Green Paper, *Quality and Choice*, to seek to change the old attitude by insisting that all references should be to 'lettings', instead of 'allocations'. The Green Paper supported the idea of introducing 'choice-based lettings' policies developed by Market Harborough District Council in Leicestershire, which itself was based on a model pioneered at Delft in the Netherlands.[2]

Following the Green Paper, the Government selected 20 local councils to develop pilot schemes to promote 'choice-based' lettings through which vacancies are advertised, both in local council offices and on the internet, and people can choose which homes to apply for. The results to date are very positive – and in some instances remarkable.

In Bradford the council set a target of increasing lettings to members of black and minority ethnic communities by at least 10 per cent a year, until they reflected the proportion in the population as a whole, as they had previously been seriously under-represented in social housing. An analysis showed that lettings to black and ethnic minority applicants increased from 10 per cent of all lettings to over 68 per cent in a year. There was also a dramatic increase in applications for council housing from that group of households as they became aware of what accommodation was available and believed that they would have a choice over which area they would live in. Previously, many Muslim families, in particular, had been deterred from moving to many council estates in the city because they would face racial hostility in the areas where they were re-housed.[3]

The results of the pilot schemes in different types of authorities show encouraging results in consumer satisfaction, as a result of much better knowledge of what accommodation is available and enabling applicants to make choices about what to bid for. They also reported a range of other benefits that have resulted from the introduction of the schemes. In the light of the success of the choice-based lettings pilots, the Government is now expecting all housing authorities and housing associations to set up such schemes.

The limit of choice-based lettings schemes, however, especially in areas where the housing stock consists primarily of high-density flats, is that only a small number of applicants can obtain the type of accommodation they want. Their choice is also limited to the properties already owned by local authorities or housing associations.

A choice to rent

A more radical idea would be for social landlords to give people an opportunity to choose where they would like to live, without limiting this to what the council or housing association already own. This is what the Ridgehill Housing Association, a stock transfer association in Hertfordshire did. With the support of the Housing Corporation, they developed the idea of a 'choice to rent'. Instead of offering the family with top priority on the housing register, the Carruthers, a vacant property that the association already owned, they invited them to go to an estate agent and choose where they would like to live. A photograph in the association's Annual Report shows a delightful picture of the two-bedroom house, with flowers blooming on the front wall, bought for £128,000 in Borehamwood. It was done within the normal Housing Corporation cost limits and more quickly than the average purchase of an existing property.[4]

The home the Carruthers chose, Ridgehill Housing Association, 2001
Ridgehill Housing Association

This type of initiative should be introduced much more widely. The primary aim of a 'choice to rent' policy is to empower tenants by giving them the opportunity to choose their home, rather than be dependent on the decision of their landlord. It has the potential to be a very liberating policy, but it could also contribute to wider strategic aims of re-structuring the pattern of housing tenure and developing more socially mixed communities.

Local councils or housing associations should offer existing tenants the opportunity to choose a new home, provided it can be purchased for no more than the selling price of their existing accommodation. In some circumstances new applicants for housing could also have the opportunity to choose the home where they wish to live, in the same way as with the Ridgehill initiative.

An example of how the policy might work is that of an older couple occupying a three bedroom council flat in an inner London borough, who would like to move out. Possible options might be a flat in outer London, or a small terraced house in a town outside London, or a bungalow by the sea. A study of the market shows that properties could be bought in each of those areas from between £150,000 and £200,000. Their current three bedroom flat could be sold for as much as £250,000.

That deal would not cost the council anything financially. However, by selling a vacant three bedroom flat it would lose a desperately needed family-sized property. A better alternative would be to re-house a family who urgently needed a transfer from an overcrowded one- or two-bedroom flat, and sell that to a first time buyer, ideally a key public-service worker needing somewhere close to their work. Even the smaller flat could be sold for the price of the property the older couple had moved to.

There would be no net capital cost to the council, but three households would have benefited – the older person moving out, the overcrowded family getting a transfer and the first time buyer.

Perhaps surprisingly, this policy could be especially relevant in high-cost areas, where there is a serious shortage of affordable housing for middle income households, and a concentration of economically inactive households in socially rented housing, especially in London and the south east. The differential in property prices between inner London and suburban or rural areas means that the policy could have a cost advantage. Since prices are so high in inner London, it is possible to buy a semi-detached house in outer London for less than the value of a council flat in the inner London area. Of course, there are constraints on what homes people can have, especially in high demand areas, but there are realistic policy options for increasing choice. Chapter 11 will look in more detail at how such a policy can be developed in London.

Chapter 10

Liverpool

A city reborn

Liverpool grew dramatically in the nineteenth century to become one of the world's great ports, the gateway from the north of England to the Atlantic and beyond. The city's first period of prosperity was based on the slave trade, but after abolition it achieved supremacy as Britain's largest port, based on three key advantages: the trading opportunities from the huge economic growth of the US, the industrial revolution in Lancashire's manufacturing districts and the safety of ships at sea because of British naval supremacy.

The city's peak was reached in the Edwardian era, with the new Pier Head and Harbour Building (1907) and the Royal Liver Building (1911), and gloried in its reputation as the 'second city of the Empire', 'the New York of Europe'.[1] During the nineteenth century the commercial wealth of the city was reflected in some of the grandest civic buildings anywhere in the world, and rich merchants built impressive town houses bordering the city centre. Yet this affluence existed cheek by jowl with appalling poverty and overcrowded slums.

During the Victorian era the poor were crowded into squalid back-to-back houses, with few windows, little ventilation and practically no daylight.

In 1836 a medical officer in Liverpool reported:

> I attended a family of 13, twelve of whom had typhus fever, without a bed in the cellar, or even without straw or

timber shavings – frequent substitutes for a bed. They lay on the floors so crowded that I could scarcely pass between them.[2]

In 1840 it was estimated that 20,000 people were living in cellars in Liverpool.[3] The group who experienced the worst living conditions were the Irish immigrants, who came in huge numbers during the nineteenth century to take labouring jobs in the Merseyside port. In 1851 it was estimated that 22 per cent of the city's populations were Irish, the most recent wave having come to escape the appalling potato famines.

Although Liverpool expanded as a cosmopolitan city it did not develop as an integrated and inclusive city, and immigrants faced persistent discrimination and barriers to social mobility. The ethnic group that has experienced the worst discrimination has been black immigrants, who came to Liverpool in significant numbers many years before the arrivals of immigrants from the black Commonwealth after the Second World War. They faced widespread discrimination in employment, hostility to inter-marriage, which was condemned as miscegenation, and treatment which Lord Gifford's inquiry into race relations in the city described as Liverpool's 'uniquely horrific' racism.[4]

The municipal housing programme

Liverpool was, however, the first provincial city to build council homes, with a tenement block of 164 dwellings completed in 1869. By the First World War it had built over 2,300 homes and had acquired and improved more than 11,000. In the inter-war years there was a major programme of new house building, including new suburban development, cottage estates built by the council and the clearance of the slums. Many of the new private homes were built outside the boundaries of the city, especially across the river in the Wirral and north towards Southport.

After the Second World War, Liverpool embarked on a huge programme of public house building, demolishing large swathes of the inner areas. Huge new housing estates were built to replace the homes lost, both within the boundaries of the city and beyond, including a large satellite town at Kirby and later a fully fledged new town at Skelmersdale. Many of the new homes were high-density, system-built estates, including tower blocks and sprawling deck access flats.

During the post-war years the city experienced a dramatic economic decline and the population fell from the peak of 831,000 in 1931 to 440,000 in 2001. During the 1960s and 1970s the city was the birthplace of the Beatles and the Mersey Sound, and the home for Liverpool Football Club as they gloried in years of success. Yet during those years it struggled to cope with the loss of jobs and acute social deprivation, with weak civic leadership, political turmoil, racial disturbances and flawed initiatives.

The housing renewal programme

Despite the scale of redevelopment, by the late 1960s there were still many thousands of unimproved terraced houses, lacking inside toilets, bathrooms and hot water. In response the council embarked on a major programme of housing improvement. The Shelter Neighbourhood Action Project (SNAP) was the flagship of the new policy, focused on the declaration of one of the first General Improvement Areas in the Granby ward in Liverpool 8. A small team of staff, backed by Shelter's publicity machine, achieved impressive results in assisting owner-occupiers to secure grants for improving their homes and encouraging housing associations to buy and renovate those properties which landlords were unwilling to improve.

In the 1970s the SNAP initiative was followed by an ambitious programme of General Improvement Areas (GIAs), and the declaration of Housing Action Areas (HAAs) in the worst areas of unimproved older housing. A leading role in rehabilitating older properties was played by two dynamic Shelter-supported housing associations, Merseyside Improved Houses and the Liverpool Housing Trust.

In the hot summer of 1981 the Toxteth area of Liverpool 8 erupted in serious racial disturbances, similar to those that took place in Brixton and Tottenham in London. In response, Michael Heseltine, the Secretary of State for the Environment in the Conservative Government, went to Liverpool and was visibly shocked by the extent of deprivation. The initiatives that followed included the creation of a Development Corporation as a vehicle for attracting private investment and channelling public funding. The results were a number of high profile projects, especially around the Albert Dock, but little impact on the inner core area where deprivation was greatest.

During the 1970s the Liberal Party gained control of the council, and strongly supported the role of housing associations as well as the growth of housing co-ops. When the militant-dominated Labour Party won control they reverted to an ambitious programme of municipal house building. This may have been an appropriate policy in the past, but by the mid 1980s it flew in the face of reality. The population was falling, there was a surplus of council housing, and priority should have been given to demolishing or renovating the huge stock of old, unimproved terraces in the city's inner core.

Transferring council housing to new landlords

By the 1990s there were a growing number of empty homes in the least popular council estates and the poor neighbourhoods of private housing.

The first major initiative to tackle the problem was the setting up of a Housing Action Trust (HAT) in 1994. The policies for creating HATs were included in the 1988 Housing Act, seen by the Conservative Government authorities as a means for putting substantial resources into problem housing estates and wresting control of council housing from local authorities. In response to opposition from tenants in some of the proposed HAT areas, however, the Government conceded that tenants should have the option of voting for a return to council ownership at the end of the life of the HAT.

In total, seven HATs were set up and each was allocated substantial funds for replacing or renovating the properties on the HAT estates. The Liverpool HAT was the largest, with the unique feature that it did not comprise a single large housing estate, but over 5,000 flats in 67 tower blocks across a wide area of the city.

When the HAT completed its life in 2005 more than £300 million had been spent, with the demolition of the old tower blocks and their replacement by low-rise new homes. All the tenants re-housed from the flats have been able to move into new homes built by housing associations on the land where the tower blocks had been.

The regeneration of Speke

One of the areas of Liverpool that had experienced severe problems was on the southern edge of the city. In the late 1940s the council built the Speke estate of over 5,000 houses for tenants moving from the overcrowded slums of the inner city. It consisted almost entirely of houses with gardens, and was initially seen as a showpiece estate, yet with the exodus of jobs in the city, the estate came to be occupied almost entirely by unemployed and non-earning tenants. The neighbouring area of Garston comprised mainly privately owned Victorian terraces. The whole area of Speke and Garston had been badly hit by the decline of the manufacturing industry and the port at Garston Docks. By the early 1990s the whole area was a neighbourhood of concentrated poverty, with an all-pervading sense of hopelessness.

Over the past decade it has benefited from an innovative and successful regeneration programme, through a tripartite partnership between the Speke Garston Development Company, the Speke Garston Partnership (SGP) and South Liverpool Housing (SLH). A key ingredient of the success has been the sequence of activity, with the first stage being the economic regeneration, which acted as a catalyst for the housing market renewal.

The Development Company brought new life into the area by redeveloping a large area of derelict land for industrial and commercial space, and attracted firms creating almost 10,000 jobs, especially in call centres, biopharmaceutical companies and the car industry. The SGP secured funding from the Single Regeneration Budget for a major programme of education and training to prepare local residents to take advantage of the new employment opportunities.

The third stage was the creation of SLH, created in 1999 to take responsibility for the Speke estate when it was transferred from the City Council, with funding for the redevelopment of the estate and building new homes. Despite the severe problems of the old Speke estate, a survey of tenants found that 83 per cent wanted to stay in the area. When asked what was wrong the most frequent response of residents was the lack of jobs. The work of the Development Company in attracting new jobs was therefore critical in persuading residents to remain. As well as the improvement to existing homes 5,000 new owner-occupied homes have been built on land adjoining the Speke estate, and these have helped to create a more balanced tenure mix in south Liverpool.

Matthew Gardiner was the Chief Executive of the South Liverpool Housing Trust for its first five years. He believes that modernising the housing was important, but the greatest challenge was to restore and build the confidence of the residents in the community. Three key aims have been to 'Engage, Inspire and Invest'. He sees the creation of a Junior Board for SLH as one of its most exciting developments. It has 15 members, aged between 12 and 18, with a wide remit to make proposals on what can be done to improve life in the community. Its real success is in 'building self-esteem' among young people who have grown up in a community with a deep-rooted sense of failure and low horizons of achievement.

During its first year all the members of the Junior Board completed the training programme, achieved a nationally recognised qualification, met regularly with the South Liverpool Housing Board, performed at two AGMs of SLH and created a Youth Delivery Plan. They also produce their own magazine, which explains the work of the Board with cleverly illustrated cartoon pictures, as well as a letter saying 'this all sounds really cool – can I start a Junior Board in my area', signed from the How Singh Authority in China.

Housing market renewal

To politicians and housing managers in the city who had always experienced people queuing for housing, the growth of void properties was profoundly disturbing. In the frenzied public debate which ensued, some put the blame on destructive behaviour by 'problem tenants', while others argued that the 'stigma of social housing' was the cause. Few people focused on the underlying causes.

The number of empty properties in Liverpool doubled from 9,692 in 1985 (5 per cent of the housing stock) to 18,666 properties in 2001 (9 per cent of the stock). Perversely, almost 12,000 additional homes were built in the city over that period, despite the evidence of falling demand and increasing voids.

What was happening in Liverpool was taking place in a number of cities and older industrial towns across the north of England. Similar stories were told of landlords finding it very difficult to let properties, existing tenants simply abandoning their homes, and owner-occupiers finding that house prices had plummeted.

The most thorough analysis of the overall problem was made by the Policy Action Team on Unpopular Housing (see Chapter 6). The most influential study of what was happening in the north west was the study of the M62 corridor from Manchester to Merseyside, carried out by a team of researchers from the Centre for Urban and Regional Studies (CURS) led by Brendan Nevin.[5] A key element in the reports produced from both these projects was the focus on the *structural causes of low demand*. The CURS report studied the housing markets across the sub-region, documenting trends in employment patterns, demographic changes and house prices.

Both reports identified the perverse impact of regional planning and national housing investment policies in accentuating the inequalities of housing supply and demand. By granting permission for new housing developments, mainly on greenfield sites, the planning authorities had encouraged people to move out of the inner urban areas.

Merseyside was one of the areas chosen by the Government for the Housing Market Renewal Initiative (HMRI) Pathfinder project described in Chapter 6. The main geographical focus for the Pathfinder is Liverpool's Inner Core, but it also extends northwards to Bootle (in the borough of Sefton) and southwards across the river to Birkenhead (in the borough of Wirral). The project covers 125,000 homes, 76,000 of them in Liverpool.

Initially, each Pathfinder project was given funding to develop a prospectus, setting out a fifteen-year strategy for developing sustainable communities that provide a good quality living environment for all residents. A key strategic aim was to increase the proportion of owner-occupied housing in the Pathfinder area so as to attract more middle and higher income residents.

The Liverpool HMRI is seeking £670 million of public funding over the full life of the project. This will be complemented by over £1,200 million of developer investment in privately owned housing. The funding will pay for the demolition of over 20,000 homes and the construction of 18,500 new homes, of which three quarters will be privately owned.

The major focus for demolitions will be the 'two up, two down' small terraced houses in the Inner Core. Liverpool has a larger proportion of terraced properties than any other city, mainly built in the nineteenth century for workers in the docks and related industries tied to the port of Liverpool and the shipyards of Birkenhead. While some of the neighbourhoods of terraced housing are stable and popular, especially those which benefited from the extensive programme of General Improvement Areas and Housing Action Areas in the 1970s, the supply of small terraced homes now exceeds the demand.

A new housing strategy

A key weakness in Liverpool for many years was the lack of strong, visionary civic leadership. One reason for this was the social geography of Merseyside, where a large proportion of the more affluent middle class have lived outside the boundaries of the city, especially in owner-occupied homes in the Wirral. Two of the outstanding leaders through the city's most difficult and turbulent years were the church leaders: the Anglican Bishop, David Sheppard, and the Roman Catholic Archbishop, Derek Worlock. In a city long divided by sectarian bitterness and social exclusion they set an inspiring example of ecumenical unity, commitment to social justice and articulate advocacy.

Yet church leaders cannot be a substitute for effective local government. For many years Liverpool suffered from the shortcomings of the City Council. It lacked any coherent strategy for tackling the massive challenges caused by the loss of jobs, falling population, poor quality housing, low educational achievement and some of the highest levels of deprivation of any area in the country.

In 1998 the Liberal Democrats gained overall control of the City Council and embarked on a bold programme of change, led by the Leader, Mike Storey, and the Deputy Leader, Richard Kemp, who was also the Executive Member for Housing, Neighbourhoods and Community Safety.

They produced a Housing Strategy identifying five zones across the city. The Eastern Fringe covers three areas, consisting largely of peripheral housing estates needing extensive redevelopment. The Southern Fringe includes the Speke estate, where South Liverpool Housing has carried out a major programme of regeneration. The Suburban Core consists predominantly of owner-occupied housing, including many semi-detached and larger terraced homes built in the first half of the twentieth century. The Inner Core surrounds the city centre in an area of concentrated deprivation. A substantial proportion of properties in the zone are old terraced properties, in poor physical condition and in low demand. This is the area where the greatest programme of demolition and building new homes is required.

Finally, between the Inner Core and Suburban Cores is the Central Buffer, where the overall condition of the housing and quality of neighbourhoods is better than in the Inner Core, but could experience market failure if action to sustain those neighbourhoods is not successful.

The strategy for the Eastern Fringe is to transfer 13,000 council homes to housing associations. Tenants voted by a large majority to the transfer of the stock, with the estates in the Netherley Valley and Dovecote estates being transferred to Riverside Housing and Croxteth, and Norris Green to the Liverpool Housing Trust. The transfer will generate £600 million for the regeneration of these homes over the next thirty years.

The council still owns and manages 19,500 homes, and this is one area where significant improvements have not been achieved. A major difficulty in achieving improvements is the long legacy of poor management, which is reflected in low standards of performance, low staff motivation and morale, and a lack of trust between tenants and the housing department.

Ken Perry is the Chief Executive of the Plus Housing Group (the new group structure which includes the Co-operative Development Services (CDS) housing association). He recalls that, when CDS took on the responsibility for management of Housing Action Trust properties, many tenants had simply stopped reporting repairs because they had no expectation that they would be carried out. He also remembers the bemused expression on the face of one young woman when faced with the expectation that she should actually pay rent for her tenancy.

The council is carrying out an options appraisal to inform its decision-making on the future of its housing stock. The council estimates that £120 million investment is needed to bring those properties up to the Decent Homes Standard. To make the improvements needed to meet tenant's expectations, including improvement to the wider estate environment, the long-term cost is estimated to be £350 million.

In practice, the only realistic option for securing the resources needed is the transfer of the housing stock to a new social landlord. The Housing Service was awarded 'no stars' as a result of the inspection by the Audit Commission, and so would not meet the standard set by the ODPM for allocating extra capital resources from setting up an Arm's Length Management Organisation.

Since 1993 almost 24,000 properties have been transferred to new social landlords, and each has resulted in large-scale investment to provide better homes and improvements in the quality of the housing service. Provided the consultation process with tenants is handled well and the potential benefits are communicated effectively, the council is confident that tenants will support proposals for transferring the remaining housing stock.

The Life model

One of the new initiatives being developed for effective delivery of the council's new strategy is the 'Life model'. This idea emerged in response to concern that there were many different agencies working in each neighbourhood, and this was resulting in duplication and confusion, both between agencies and for residents.

The Life model sets our four roles, with each agency having a clearly defined function in every area where it is active:

- **Lead** in an area
- **Influence** what happens in an area or part of it
- **Follow** – collaborate in delivering the direction set by others
- **Exit** an area.

What this means for the Plus Housing Group, as an example of how the Life model works in practice, is that it has the **lead** role in two main pathfinder areas for the Housing Market Renewal Initiative, and it has the **influence** role in another of the HMRI areas. Where it has a presence in other parts of the HMRI it will **follow**, so as to collaborate in helping to deliver where the lead is set by another agency. Where it role is minimal, it will where appropriate hand over its work to another agency and **exit**.

Include

The Include model has been developed as an innovative way of providing holistic neighbourhood management. It was set up in 2001, as a joint venture between the Plus Housing Group and the City Council to bring together all the agencies involved in providing services in the Liverpool 8 area. Include has brought together staff from all the key statutory, housing association and voluntary agencies in the same offices, pooled budgets from what were previously multiple funding sources, and radically overhauled the way investment is allocated in the area.

The Plus Housing Group review of 2003/4 is buoyant about the achievements over the first three years:

> The impact has been staggering. Crime rates have fallen dramatically (between 50–85 per cent); property prices have stabilized and increased in excess of the regional and national average. The result is that L8 is now experiencing a renaissance. Community confidence is growing and businesses and residents are choosing to stay and return to the area in increasing numbers.[6]

The rebirth of the city

After a long period of economic decline Liverpool has started to achieve a remarkable regeneration, and in 2003 the population increased for the first time in seventy years. European regional funds have created new jobs, the Albert Docks riverfront has been transformed, The Tate gallery has opened. A major new City Centre Development is taking place in the Paradise Street area, with the Grosvenor Group investing £800 million to provide retail space for several flagship development stores and over 90 shops, as well as a million square feet of mixed-use development including a new bus station and over 300 new homes. Probably the most significant event in raising the confidence of the city is being chosen as the European City of Culture in 2008, and an ambitious programme of activity is being planned to mark this, spread across the whole community.

The past twenty years have been extraordinarily difficult for the community leaders who have been struggling to stem the seemingly unstoppable tide of economic decline and social disintegration. Huge credit is due to those in many public, private and voluntary agencies who have sought to find new ways forward in securing sustainable regeneration.

An important role has been played by the housing associations in Liverpool. Liverpool Improved Homes was formed in 1928 but its rapid growth only began in the late 1960s, when it became one of the first Shelter-supported housing associations and played a key role in the city's housing renewal programmes and subsequently began developing new-build projects. For over thirty years its chief executive was Barry Natton, who led its expansion into the Riverside Group, one of the largest social landlords in the country. He was succeeded by Deborah Shackleton, who had been the Development Director of CDS for over ten years before coming to Riverside in 1992. Although the Riverside Group now has over 40,000 properties in the midlands and north west, its largest presence is still in Liverpool, where it owns 7,000 properties in the older areas of the city. It has a lead role in the HMRI Heartland areas, as well as taking over the former council housing estates in the Dovecote and Netherley Valley area of the Eastern Fringe.

The Liverpool Housing Trust was formed in 1965 and became one of the first Shelter-supported housing associations. The Trust owns 10,000 homes across Merseyside, with 5,000 of these within the city of Liverpool. It has also played a leading role in Liverpool's housing renewal and new housing developments, and is the lead agency in one of the HMRI areas and in taking over the council's housing stock in the Croxteth and Norris Green area of the Eastern Fringe. For over twenty-five years its Chief Executive has been David Bebb, who, like Barry Natton, has played a leading role in the National Housing Federation, the representative body for housing associations, also both were Chair of the NHF for four years.

Richard Kemp was a young Liberal councillor in the 1970s, who supported the first new-build housing co-operatives. Since

1997 he has played a leading role in the development of the council's housing and neighbourhood development strategy, as well as holding senior positions nationally in the Local Government Association. In 2004 he became the Chair of the Plus Housing Group. Two of his key beliefs are that housing policies must be linked to a wider vision of the city, and responsibility should be devolved to local communities.

He recalls the mistake the council made in the Anfield area, where it encountered fierce opposition from local residents to plans that included the demolition of 900 properties. In response the council gave money to local community organisations to enable them to draw up proposals. After two years of extensive consultation with residents, they came forward with proposals which included reducing the number of two up, two down terraced houses and the number of flats, building more homes for sale, helping low-income owners to preserve the equity in their homes by moving to new properties, and demolishing over 1,000 homes. The change in the community's views had come from being able to make an informed assessment of the alternative options and, most importantly, take responsibility for shaping the future of their area.

What is happening in Liverpool should be recognised as encouraging evidence that regeneration strategies can be successful in urban areas that have suffered from massive employment losses and acute social deprivation. A key element has been the link between the strategies for creating and attracting new jobs, the programmes for education and training and the plans for housing renewal. All three are critical for persuading existing residents to stay in Liverpool and attracting new people to come. The type of housing and balance of tenure must be appropriate to the aspirations and incomes of different groups, in order to provide a range of homes in different tenures where people want to live.

Chapter 11

London
A world city

During the nineteenth century the population of London grew from one million to over seven million people. It became not only the largest city in the world, but much greater than any city in history.

During the twentieth century there were three major phases to London's development. The first phase came between the two world wars as London's population continued to grow, reaching a peak of 8.7 million in 1938. However, the *population* growth was dwarfed by the *spatial* expansion, made possible by the extension of the underground and bus services to the edges of outer London.

During those twenty years London doubled in physical size on the ground. In total, 860,000 new homes were built, an average of 40,000 homes a year, mostly new homes built for sale. The new homes were predominantly semi-detached houses with gardens, built at a density of 12 houses per acre, which was much lower than the densities in inner London. There was a huge growth of the suburbs, ranging across the whole of outer London from Croydon, Bromley and Wimbledon to the south; Twickenham, Ealing and Southall to the west; Edgware, Hendon and Enfield to the north; and Ilford, Chingford and Upminster to the east, with new suburban neighbourhoods springing up in almost every area of outer London.

During the inter-war years the London County Council built a quarter of a million homes in the suburbs. However, 90,000 of these were built on the huge development at the Becontree estate at Barking and Dagenham, which were not in the same area as middle class housing. After the completion of Becontree, further efforts by the LCC to continue what was termed 'out-county development' became increasingly controversial, as existing residents protested against the arrival of working class neighbours and local authorities tried to block the LCC's land acquisition programme. Unwilling to confront the opposition with the use of compulsory purchase powers, the LCC resorted to 'secret acquisitions in lower class suburbs where the voices of protest were less powerful'.[1]

An extraordinary instance of class hatred was the saga of the Downham wall, echoing the events in the battle over the Cutteslowe Wall in Oxford described in Chapter 1. In order to minimise everyday contact between the council tenants and the 'respectable residents' of Bromley, local citizens built a wall to prevent contact with tenants of the new LCC estate built on the edge of the neighbouring borough of Lewisham, just inside the LCC boundary. Bromley Council waged a lengthy legal battle against the LCC who sought to have the wall demolished, but it stood for many years.[2]

The counties of Hertfordshire, Kent and Surrey virtually excluded the LCC from their territories. In the words of one Hertfordshire county councillor: 'we are deeply opposed to having the thin edge of the wedge brought in by any shape or form that will bring the LCC's claws upon us'.[3]

One consequence of this opposition was that most of the LCC housing estates after 1930 were built in inner London, predominantly in the Labour controlled boroughs in south east and east London, which were willing to make sites available for council housing. There was a marked impact on the concentration of poverty in that area of London as low-income tenants increasingly occupied those estates.

After the Second World War

In 1944 Sir Patrick Abercrombie's Plan for Greater London was published. This set out an ambitious and comprehensive plan for post-war construction, re-building the areas destroyed by war damage and tackling the massive shortage of homes. The Plan included proposals for a network of new towns, beyond the green belt, to accommodate London's overspill.

However, to the dismay of the garden city movement, who were advocates of lower density development, the Plan proposed a new hierarchy of housing densities, which required building for 200 persons per acre in the most central areas and 136 persons per acre in rest of inner London. In outer London the proposed density of 50 persons per acre was similar to that for most of the semi-detached suburban homes and the council housing 'cottage estates' built in the inter-war years at 12 houses per acre. The Plan recommended that only flats should be built on land in the inner areas.

Between 1945 and 1980 huge areas of inner London were redeveloped. Yet instead of this bringing economic and social prosperity, much of inner London experienced traumatic economic decline and population exodus. Manufacturing jobs disappeared, the ports closed, and skilled manual and white-collar workers migrated from inner London. The people left behind were mostly the unskilled and non-working, increasingly clustered on council estates.

Some of the early post-war development such as the Alton estate in Roehampton, the Churchill Gardens estate in Pimlico, and the Golden Lane estate in Clerkenwell were attractive architect-designed estates, which became showpiece models of public housing, visited by municipal architects and planners from across the world. Sadly by the 1950s the industrialised building methods came into fashion, and were embraced whole-heartedly by the LCC and its successor the Greater London Council (GLC), as well as most inner London councils. In total 68,500 flats of 10 storeys or more were built in London.

The key element in the decentralisation policy envisaged by the Labour Government and the post-war planners was the creation of the new towns. Over the next forty years the first wave of eight new towns started in 1946 grew to accommodate 424,000 people. The second tranche of twelve 'expanded towns' added an extra 120,000. The third generation of new towns at Milton Keynes, Northampton and Peterborough added a further 180,000 people by the mid 1980s. Milton Keynes became the fastest-growing area in Britain and by 2003 had a population of a quarter of a million.

However, voluntary movement out of London dwarfed this planned migration. Even in the peak years of new town development in the 1960s this exceeded planned overspill by a ratio of two to one. In the five years from 1966 to 1971 alone, an estimated half a million people moved out of the working class areas of inner London, 47 per cent to outer London and 34 per cent to the Home Counties. Most were skilled manual and office workers moving to buy a house. It was predominantly the poor who stayed, including low paid workers, older people, and single parents.

From the early 1950s London began to experience a new period of inward migration. Over many generations people have come to London from other countries, sometimes to flee from persecution, more often in search of work and attracted by the possibilities offered by one of the world's leading cities.

Most of the new wave of immigrants came from countries of the black Commonwealth, initially from the West Indies, then from Nigeria, India, Pakistan and later from Bangladesh and other countries. Large numbers also came from Cyprus, partly as a result of the long-running conflict between Greece and Turkey. Newcomers faced serious problems finding accommodation. Despite the large-scale housing programmes, many council lettings were going to tenants displaced by redevelopment.

Black people consistently faced discrimination from landlords. As a result many were forced to pay high rents to live in run-down multi-occupied properties in Notting Hill, Paddington, Brixton, Hackney, Tower Hamlets and elsewhere in inner London. By the 1970s, as allocation policies were reformed to give higher priority to housing need, many more black families were re-housed by local authorities and housing associations, although disproportionately in flats on the less popular estates.

A new development was the growth of 'gentrification' in inner London, especially in the Victorian street properties which had escaped the bulldozer in the era of clearance and redevelopment. From the 1960s a growing number of middle class families bought and renovated houses, initially in areas such as Islington, Camden, north Kensington, Fulham, Battersea, and then increasingly across almost every area where there were Victorian terraced properties to be found.

In the 1970s the new generation of housing associations were also buying houses for renovation in some of these areas, and some local authorities also embarked on 'municipalisation' programmes to acquire street properties. In some instances this was by compulsory purchase where landlords were failing to carry out improvements, or were threatening tenants with eviction. More generally the aim was to increase the supply of social rented housing in order to house people in severe housing need.

In his study, *London in the Twentieth Century*, Jerry White makes the pertinent comment that:

> The combination in the same street of owner occupation and private renting, mixed with some council-owned 'street' properties, proved a more dynamic, adaptive and tolerant environment than the council estate. The mixture of classes seemed to make it easier to cope with a mixture of races, too.[4]

Developments after 1980

From the early 1980s the long decline in London's population was reversed. The population of 6.9 million in 1981 was 2 million people fewer than the peak population of 1938. By 2001 it had risen to 7.4 million, and is projected to rise to over 8 million by 2011.

Since the early 1980s London's economy has been booming as new jobs have been created, especially in financial services, information technology, the media and tourism. Yet over

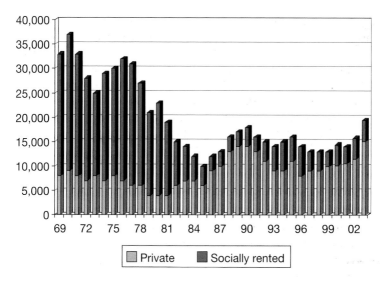

Graph 11.1 Number of new homes built in London

this period the number of homes being built in London fell sharply.

The post-war peak of new homes being built in London was in 1970 when 37,000 new homes were built, including 28,000 homes for rent built by local authorities or housing associations. From the early 1980s this fell to an annual level of under 15,000, with fewer than 5,000 being built for rent.

Over this period London became a more divided city. The gap between supply and demand pushed up house prices. Widening income inequalities enabled the better-off to pay higher prices for their homes. The rising value of property encouraged people to buy residential property as investments, including second homes, business flats and *pieds-à-terre* which were not even lived in for much of the year.

The dark side of the boom was the worsening problem faced by the less well-off. Two groups of people experienced the crisis most severely. Chapter 7 has described the growth in the number of homeless families in temporary accommodation.

Less recognised, but at least as desperate, has been the massive growth in overcrowding, especially among council tenants. According to the 1991 and 2001 censuses, overcrowding in London, defined as households living at a density of more than one person per room, rose by 20 per cent. Severe overcrowding, defined as households living with more than one and a half person per room, increased by almost 50 per cent, reversing the long trend of falling levels of overcrowding.

In 2001 there were 150,000 households (5 per cent of all households) that were overcrowded, and 61,000 households (2 per cent of the total) that were *severely* overcrowded. Families with children experience overcrowding most acutely, especially larger families. There are 460,000 children in London living in homes with too few rooms. Research has shown that overcrowding can damage both the physical and emotional development of children, and is linked to the frequency of infectious diseases, especially tuberculosis. It also has a harmful effect on educational development, particularly by making home study more difficult.

There has also been a marked shift in the incidence of overcrowding in different tenures. Between 1991 and 2001 overcrowding *doubled* among council tenants in London, exceeding for the first time the rate of overcrowding experienced by private tenants.

There are also striking differences between ethnic groups. Overcrowding is three times more common among minority ethnic households than white British households. Bangladeshi households are five times more likely than white British households to be overcrowded. The boroughs with the highest levels of overcrowding are primarily those with large minority ethnic populations, particularly Tower Hamlets, Newham, Hackney, Brent, Southwark and Hackney. There are also very acute problems of overcrowding in Westminster and in Kensington and Chelsea, where the low stock of social housing reduces the re-housing possibilities.

It is hard to convey the desperation caused by the most severe overcrowding, for example where families of eight or more are crowded in a two bedroom flat, with no prospect of re-housing in larger accommodation. Karen Buck, the Labour MP whose constituency covers North Kensington and Paddington, has seen the problems of severe overcrowding get worse since she was elected in 1997, and believes that it is the greatest problem faced by her constituents. She has described the conditions experienced by a few of those families, who came to her as their constituency MP in November 2004. Sadly they are only a small proportion of the families facing desperate overcrowding in her constituency alone:

> Ms P is bringing her three children up in a 1 bedroom flat, which is also up three flights of stairs. An environmental health assessment carried out early in 2004 stated that 'we have to accept that the living room can be used as a bedroom and a child between one and 10 only counts as half a unit (a child under one does not count at all)'. Therefore, in this case, there are 2½ units occupying the flat . . . therefore the flat is not overcrowded within the meaning of the legislation.

> The E family are of Iranian origin, but are British citizens of long standing. Four of them now share a 1 bedroom flat, where the most serious problem is their five year old son, who is both an insulin-dependent diabetic and autistic. The consultant psychiatrist says 'such a cramped environment would be difficult for any family, but given M's severe health problems the current accommodation adds to the stress the parents are under . . . children with Autistic spectrum disorder particularly dislike crowded restrictive environments and need space to minimise their behaviour difficulty'.

> Mrs J, who is sharing a 1 bedroom flat with her husband and three children, aged 8, 5 and 9 months, has just been assessed as being statutorily overcrowded. Because of this, the family will gain vital extra points to enable them to go to the top of the list for a 3 bedroom flat. Unfortunately,

Westminster Council told me at the same time that as 'they had allocated all the 3 bedroom flats they expected to for the year', they must wait until the next financial year before they are even in with a chance of a new home.

Mrs H's overcrowding case was brought to the attention of Kensington Council in 2000, but as of November 2004, she had still not been re-housed. One of the children suffers from Sickle Cell disease and is in almost constant pain, yet must sleep on the floor of his mother's room on a blow up bed. The clinical nurse writes 'I have to write to you (the council) on not only health but humanitarian grounds. . . . I would like to emphasise my concerns regarding this mother's mental and physical health and her ability to carry on meeting the needs of her children in this intolerable environment.'

Back in 2001, the D family's health visitor wrote in support of their re-housing, saying that they needed a move to a larger and level-access property as a matter of urgency. She said 'C (now four years old) was born with multiple chronic health conditions. Mrs D's current accommodation is a 2 bedroom flat on the 4th floor, up 70 steep winding stairs with no lift. . . . The stress on the whole family and total disruption of family life is beyond bearing . . . Mrs D is now on sick leave with severe anaemia, physical and psychological stress.' As of November 2004, they were living in the same condition.

Mrs O lives in a 1 bedroom flat with a three year old son who has epilepsy, which causes nocturnal fits resulting in bedwetting. He sleeps in a cot next to his baby brother. A letter from a member of the Sure Start team states 'There is no gap between the three beds. In addition, J has had epileptic attacks while on the stairs to the flat, and has fallen down and knocked himself unconscious . . . all these problems are causing depression and are making the mother very angry and frustrated with the lack of response to her difficulties.'[5]

Less acute, though much more widely recognised, are the housing needs of people with moderate incomes who have been facing growing difficulties in finding a home, especially those who want to buy. They could afford without difficulty to buy a home in most areas of Britain, but find it impossible in the overheated London housing market.

Those most affected include key workers, especially teachers, nurses, bus drivers and those employed in the running of essential services. For many of them it is important to have homes close to their jobs, especially those working in 24-hour services such as hospitals. Both the health and education services are experiencing serious problems recruiting and retaining staff, who have no problems in moving to jobs in other areas of the country where housing is much cheaper yet salaries not greatly lower.

The new London Plan

During the 1980s and 1990s London badly needed a new Strategic Plan. Yet nothing happened. The Conservative Government abolished the Greater London Council in 1986 and for the next fifteen years there was no democratically elected body for London. As the Mayor's consultative report, *Towards a London Plan*, said:

> Without its own strategic authority London developed without a systematic vision of its place within the UK economy. Demands placed on London by rapid economic growth have not been matched by increases in the supply of homes.[6]

Shortly after his election in May 2000 Ken Livingstone appointed an independent Housing Commission to assess the need for affordable homes in London and make proposals on how these could be provided. The Commission invited written evidence and met with representatives of a wide range of agencies, and members visited projects to see at first hand the problems and new solutions which were being developed.

The Commission's report, *Homes for a World City*,[7] proposed new policies in three key areas. First, its assessment of housing need included the backlog of existing unmet housing need, in addition to the projected demand from newly forming households. The result was the estimate that London needed 43,000 new homes for each of the next fifteen years; 32,000 in order to meet new demand and 11,000 to tackle the backlog. As a result of the different methodology, the estimate was significantly higher than the assessment in the previous regional planning guidance and almost three times the number of new homes being built.

Second, the Commission identified what it termed an 'intermediate' housing market for people on moderate incomes. Much of the debate on this issue has focused on the needs of so-called 'key workers', most commonly defined as nurses and teachers. While in the short term it may be right to focus on the urgent need to recruit and retain staff for these jobs, similar difficulties are experienced by staff in other essential services, such as fire fighters and paramedics, staff in transport and local government, and also by people working in the retail, tourist and service industries which are vital to London's economy. The Commission's report stressed the need to develop a much wider range of 'housing products' – discounted home ownership, shared equity, sub-market renting – for people in that wide group who fall between the stools of full market and social rented housing.

The third, and most controversial, recommendation was that the London Plan should include the requirement that 50 per cent of all new homes should be 'affordable'. This was defined as housing for people on low or moderate incomes who cannot afford general market housing, whether to buy or to rent. The Commission proposed that 35 per cent of all new homes should be socially rented housing for people on low incomes, and 15 per cent for the intermediate market. The Commission also stressed the importance of developing mixed tenure housing, and promoting socially mixed communities across all areas of London.

The Mayor's *Draft London Plan*, published in May 2002, recognised the seriousness of the housing difficulties in London and set out a comprehensive range of polices for tackling these. Many of the housing policies were based on the recommendations made by the Housing Commission, including the target that 50 per cent of all new homes should be affordable.[8]

The weakness in the Draft Plan was the target for building new homes. Lower projections of the number of new households had reduced the demand from 43,000 to 31,900 homes, but the Plan only proposed a target of building 'at least 23,000' homes each year.

The publication of the Draft Plan was followed by a consultation period, during which written responses could be submitted, and an Examination in Public (EIP) was held before a Panel of independent inspectors. The formal sessions of the EIP enabled representatives of the Mayor and invited participants to discuss key issues from the Plan, following which the Panel prepared their report.

The week-long discussion of the housing policies of the Plan, held in April 2003, contained sharp differences of view between participants, but concluded with surprisingly wide agreement on key issues. This included the views that the 23,000 target was too low, and the need was for 30,000 new homes a year, and the acceptance by the house builders and developers that a 50 per cent target of affordable housing was achievable, provided the private sector contribution was matched by an adequate input of public subsidy.

The Panel's report was published in July 2003, including the findings that:

> The Examination in Public's testing has shown the figure of 23,000 is likely to be an under-provision against probable need. It is inconsistent with the stated aim of accommodating London's growth within its own boundaries. . . . The Panel therefore recommends that it should be amended to provide that the Mayor will seek the maximum provision

of additional housing in London towards achieving an output of 30,000 homes per year over a ten year period.

The approach to meeting the backlog of unmet need is important . . . What is clear in the London case is that unmet need, estimated by the Housing Commission at 112,000 represents a large and growing historic need which includes people who have had housing problems for many years.[9]

The recommendations of the Panel are very significant. It is the first time that a target of 50 per cent of new homes should be affordable has been accepted by an independent Planning Inspector. It is also the first time that the requirement to tackle the backlog of need has been so firmly endorsed.

The new target for 30,000 new homes a year is significantly higher than the 'minimum of 23,000' in the Draft Plan. Achieving it will be difficult and will require the use of all appropriate sites, including higher densities where this is consistent with the criteria for sustainable residential quality. The target for affordable housing also depends on the Housing Corporation being given adequate funding by the Government for supporting the development of affordable housing, as well as success by the borough councils in negotiating Section 106 agreements. If this is not achieved, it will be essential to provide more of the planned growth outside London, despite the Mayor's reluctance to do this and the likely resistance of the local authorities in the surrounding regions.

The Mayor's introduction to the Draft London Plan argued that:

The fundamental strategic direction taken in the London Plan is to accommodate London's growth within the Greater London boundaries without encroaching on the green belt and other green spaces.

In the past, governments have pursued a policy of dispersal of population to new towns beyond the green belt and other regions of the country. However, London is,

Bramley G → (1994) An Affordable Crisis ..

(Housing Studies, 9(1)

European Housing

Loan Receipt
Liverpool John Moores University
Learning and Information Services

Borrower ID:	21111133704114
Loan Date:	02/02/2009
Loan Time:	4:27 pm

Introducing social policy /
11101074102t

Due Date: 09/02/2009 23:59

Please keep your receipt
in case of dispute

with New York and Tokyo, one of the three world cities. It is the financial centre of Europe and the economic hub of the UK. Any attempts to hold back London's growth, by denying it the necessary resources to maintain competitiveness or adopting policies that choke its development, would degrade the economic efficiency of the city, decrease the quality of life of Londoners and damage its environment. Expansion of London into its surrounding regions, the path chosen during much of the nineteenth and twentieth century, would be environmentally unacceptable, particularly for the surrounding regions, and is ruled out by current government policy.

Ken Livingstone expressed his views with almost evangelical fervour, repudiating the philosophy on dispersal and overspill that was the cornerstone of the Abercrombie plan and the post-war strategy. Yet if too few homes are available to house London's rising population, the people who pay the price will be those who are poorly housed or become homeless.

While the green belt has played a valuable role in restricting London's outward expansion into the countryside, it includes a lot of low quality land of no useful economic, recreational or environmental purpose, which could be used for new homes. As has been shown earlier in the book, defences of the countryside are simply a cloak for selfish nimbyism.

London's successful bid to host the 2012 Olympics is yet another factor that increases the pressure on London's housing. The prospect of the Games is likely to attract people to move to London, especially young people.

The policies in the London Plan are important and welcome. However, the London Plan is a strategy for *spatial development*. It is not an overall *housing strategy* for London. New policies are needed for acquiring or building more social rented housing in outer London and in the home counties in order to enable those low-income non-economically active tenants who want to move from housing estates in inner London. It is through policies such as these that accommodation for public service workers, and other younger people with jobs, will be freed up.

A radical new strategy

In June 2004 the Prime Minister's Strategy Unit produced an important, although largely unnoticed, *London Analytical Report*, followed by the final *London Project Report*. The Prime Minister and Deputy Prime Minister commissioned the project to consider the long-term issues facing London and its role as a capital city and world city.

The interim report warned that

> if historic trends continue, new households will significantly exceed new dwellings. Pressure on housing is a particular problem for London's public sector and key workers, who have less purchasing power than their private sector counterparts and lower purchasing power means that public sector workers have less choice over where to live. . . . There may be serious consequences if the wage gap continues to rise. There are already recruitment and retention problems in key public services'.[10]

The final report includes the conclusion that:

> London's economic comparative advantage is rooted in its ability to attract and retain a workforce that make its knowledge-based, creative and cultural economy internationally competitive.
>
> However, London has great deprivation as well as wealth and opportunity, making it the most unequal region of the UK. The Government encourages social inclusion both for its own sake and to build a stable and secure society.

It also includes the recommendation that the Government should:

> Explore options that could release some of the equity tied into the housing stock in London to fund more sustainable communities.[11]

While it does not spell out how this might be done, the report is an indication that there may be support by the Government for radical new policies.

As London's economy has changed, there has been a growing mismatch between the skills needed for jobs in inner London and the ability of people living in those areas to offer them. While growing numbers of young people seek affordable accommodation close to their jobs, much of the housing is occupied by unskilled manual workers, retired people, people with disabilities, and single mothers with young children.

The *London Project Report* puts forward the idea of offering tenants a cash incentive to move away from areas of high demand. For some earning households this might enable them to buy a home, whether in shared ownership or the full equity.

Realising some of the high potential value of inner London property would allow imaginative options for tenants and the public sector. This might include considering how the equity tied into some homes could be used to assist tenants who want to move away from areas of high demand. This might also include increased support for regeneration schemes that release equity to fund local regeneration, for example, raising densities on sites so as simultaneously mix tenures and raise private funds.

Also completed in July 2004 was the report of the London Housing Board Task Force, *Sustainable Communities: Mobility and Choice*. The remit of the Task Force was to examine key policy questions for the London Housing Strategy, including:

- Should the next Strategy promote a long-term shift in housing provision, with a more even balance of social housing across London?
- Should there be greater opportunities for key workers and people on intermediate incomes to live closer to their work?

- Given that some social housing is in high-value locations, would developing new intermediate/private sector housing on these sites unlock funding that could be used to provide a greater volume of social housing elsewhere and therefore reduce local authority waiting lists?
- Is there a case for encouraging more inter-regional mobility? If so, how can people be encouraged to consider a move away from London, and how can this be made an attractive proposition for other regions?[12]

The Task Force put forward a wide range of recommendations, including proposals for the development of private housing to cross-subsidise the refurbishment of social housing and the development of a pan-London approach to facilitating choice-based mobility.

In July 2005 the London Housing Board published *Capital Homes: The London Housing Strategy, 2005–2016*, following extensive consultation with key stakeholders.[13]

This reports the progress that has been made since the launch of the London Plan, including a significant growth in the number of new homes completed, which have increased from 14,000 in 2001/2 to 24,000 in 2004/5. However, it also reports the finding from the GLA's 2004 Housing Requirements Study which estimated that 35,400 new homes a year are needed between 2002 and 2012 to meet the existing backlog and to meet the projected growth in households, which is greater than in the previous estimate as a result of higher inward migration.

In July 2005 the Mayor published an updated *Housing Capacity Study*, based on extensive research into potential sites for house-building by the London boroughs. The important conclusion is that the total capacity for new homes for the ten-year period 2007/8 to 2016/17 is 315,327, equivalent to 31,533 a year. This is a substantial increase of 10,000 homes a year above the estimate included in the London Plan, and even higher than the 'aspirational' target of 30,000 homes.[14] The findings of the study significantly improve the prospects of meeting

– or more closely reaching – the target of new homes needed in London over the next 10 years.

The strategy includes a range of proposals for tackling over-crowding, including extending or deconverting existing socially rented homes and encouraging under-occupiers of social rented homes to move to smaller properties. It asks the Housing Corporation to target 35 per cent of its investment allocation for 2006/8 on homes with three or more bedrooms and to apply new criteria of measuring the number of *people* housed, rather than the number of *units* produced, in order to remove the perceived obstacle to providing larger homes.

The Housing Strategy also sets out the Board's proposed priorities for housing investment. These include the proposal that investment should be measured by the number of people housed, rather than units completed, so as to increase the number of larger homes; and that there should be a shift towards producing more social housing in outer London.

There is now the potential for radical new policies to re-shape the social geography of London. These could simultaneously achieve a better link between homes and jobs, especially for young people working in expanding private sector jobs and key public services; increase choice for tenants, especially non-earning households willing to move from inner areas; and promote more socially mixed communities across both outer and inner London.

The strategy can reverse the trends dating from the end of the nineteenth century. While aspiring middle class and skilled working class households were able to move to outer suburbs and out of London, unskilled and non-earning households have had no choice but to live in inner London, many in neighbourhoods of high-density flatted estates.

Some residents in those areas live there by choice, with networks of family, friends and strong local connections. However, many residents, especially tenants of social landlords, stay in inner London because they have no other choice. Private housing in outer London and outside London is unaffordable to anyone with a low income.

There is huge potential for the kind of new policies outlined in previous chapters of the book. Chapter 8 encourages social landlords to develop strategic plans for selling properties on existing housing estates and buy more terraced and semi-detached houses from private owners. Chapter 9 includes proposals enabling tenants to choose a home where they would prefer to live, provided it can be purchased for no more than the cost of their present accommodation.

One example of how this might work is in the area where the opening of the Channel Tunnel link at St Pancras and the development of the Kings Cross railway land will provide the biggest development opportunity in central London for many years. Camden Council have drawn up a strategic planning framework, with policies for a high quality, mixed use development, including 1,000 new homes, of which 50 per cent must be affordable.

That approach is consistent with the recommendations of the Mayor's Housing Commission and Draft London Plan, but the danger is that the end result will be a fragmented and unbalanced community. Half the new housing will be occupied by owner-occupiers in expensive executive homes, a third by low-income families and single people in rented homes, and 15 per cent by key workers, especially in public services. However, this is likely to be the only housing accessible to people on middle incomes.

Surrounding the new development will be the housing estates of Somers Town, Kings Cross and Caledonian Road. These are some of the most deprived neighbourhoods in inner London, with many residents who are retired, unable to work or without the skills to compete for the new jobs that will be created.

Re-structuring the pattern of housing tenure could be a way of developing a more socially balanced community, as well as extending choice and enabling more people to live close to where they work. A first step would be to ask all the current tenants, especially non-earning households, if they would like to move to a rented home away from the area – and if so enable them to choose where they would like to live.

The flats freed up could be used for people who need affordable homes close to their work – such as staff working in the 24-hour services generated by the new station and nurses, porters and doctors at University College Hospital. More radically still, the local councils might decide to sell some of the flats on the estates where people move out, on the open market and use the money to buy street properties elsewhere in the borough – or even in an area of outer London.

Over 800,000 households in London are renting from councils and housing associations, the great majority of them people on low incomes. These tenants have no alternative to social rented housing, but only a small proportion have jobs which depend on them living in homes in London.

The most recent Household Survey found that 35 per cent of residents would move out of London if they could, including 38 per cent in the lowest income bands.[15] The old Greater London Council Countryside and Seaside Homes scheme is a notable example of how successful such a scheme can be. Over a number of years the GLC acquired or built 5,000 homes for older tenants to move out of their existing dwellings. Many of these were bungalows by the sea, while others were houses or flats in all parts of the country. The scheme was enormously popular, but sadly ended with the abolition of the GLC in 1986.

The recent experience of the London boroughs 'LAWN' scheme (London Authorities with the North) has surprised many sceptics by showing that significant numbers of tenants – as well as homeless families – are willing to move to homes in 'low demand' areas in the Midlands and north. It is likely that a scheme, which made it possible for tenants to have a wider choice of where they would like to live, would be very popular.

One of the proposals of the Mayor's Commission in London was to aim for a better balance of owner-occupied and socially rented housing in London. At present, five London boroughs have over 40 per cent of their housing that is socially rented. Thirteen have between 20 per cent and 39 per cent. Fifteen have less than 20 per cent, all of them outer London boroughs.

Those boroughs with most social housing are also those with the greatest deprivation. There are powerful arguments for increasing the share of rented housing in outer London, especially by acquiring more street properties; reducing the share in some areas close to the centre; and giving priority to providing more affordable homes for people working in key public service jobs.

What could be done is to develop an integrated initiative which brings together the different proposals for tackling homelessness and overcrowding, providing more homes for key workers and developing socially diverse, mixed tenure communities across all areas of London.

The aim should be to acquire homes to rent either in outer London or in areas outside London for three groups: existing council or housing association tenants who want to move because of overcrowding in their existing accommodation; tenants who want to move out of inner London by choice; and families in temporary accommodation who need a permanent home.

Implementing the programme

Stage 1 Groups of (say) 500 households should be asked to choose the area where they would like to live, and the type of property. If properties in that area or of that type are deemed too expensive, they should be asked to choose a cheaper area or type of property. An agreement should be reached with each household on the brief for the property search.

Stage 2 A specification should be drawn up for identifying and acquiring properties that match the requirements, with a total budget for the cost of purchase and any repair/renovation costs needed to make it fit for letting. A tender brief should be produced, setting out how the work is to be carried out and specifying the skills required from a successful contractor, and tenders invited.

Stage 3 The contractors selected should identify a pool of properties that match the specification, including any appropriate properties chosen by individuals, and consult with each participant on the suitability of the properties identified. Each household should be invited to visit potential acquisitions, and give a report with their views. Where anyone is not satisfied further work should be done to identify potential properties. Offers should be made on the properties accepted as suitable, and arrangements made to complete the purchase where offers are accepted.

Stage 4   A report on proposed purchases should be submitted to the existing landlord, who will be responsible for reaching agreement on which landlord should be responsible for managing the property, and making arrangement for the letting arrangements, including any assistance needed in making the move.

Stage 5   Decisions should be made by the existing landlords on the properties vacated. The options might include re-letting in the normal way; letting at market or sub-market rents; selling on a shared equity basis; or selling outright. Whatever arrangements are proposed would need to be compatible with the funding arrangements for the programme, so as to ensure that the required capital receipts and/or higher rental income are generated.

Building a less divided city

The London Plan is an important step forward in providing a strategic housing plan, in particular the target that 50 per cent of new homes must be affordable for people who cannot pay the full market price of housing in London, the policy for developing socially balanced communities and the requirement that all boroughs must meet the targets in the Plan.

What are needed are policies that assess the demand for different types of housing, its geographical distribution, the scale of public funding needed and how it should be used.

It has been almost universally accepted that London's housing problems are so severe that there is no prospect of solving them in the foreseeable future. That assumption is defeatist, and stems from a failure to imagine radical new ways of reforming the housing market so as to satisfy better the aspirations of those wanting to rent and wanting to buy.

If the Mayor and the London boroughs work together with the Government and other key agencies it will be possible to make significant progress within five years. Tenants who want to move outside London will be able to do so, wherever possible actually choosing not just the area, but the actual homes where they would like to live. The properties freed up can be sold outright or on a shared ownership or equity basis to medium-income workers, especially people whose jobs make it essential to live in inner London. Overcrowded and homeless families will also be given priority in access to dwellings as they become available, so that it is no longer necessary to keep homeless families in temporary accommodation except in emergencies and while appropriate accommodation and support are arranged.

Chapter 12

Oases of excellence

This chapter describes a few outstanding examples of dreams that have been turned into reality. They include well-designed homes in successful, mixed tenure communities; housing co-operatives controlled by their resident members; and local communities who have campaigned to gain control over the future of their homes and neighbourhoods. The backgrounds are very different, but what they have in common is a vision of homes and communities where people are proud to live.

New Earswick, York

New Earswick was the model village on the edge of York developed by the Rowntree Village Trust (later renamed the Joseph Rowntree Housing Trust), founded by Joseph Rowntree and his sons. Their awareness of the extent of the need for a 'showcase' community was strengthened by the findings from the Survey of Poverty in York which Seebohm Rowntree conducted in 1900. This study showed the dreadful overcrowding and unsanitary conditions experienced by poor families.

The decision to build the village of New Earswick was made by Seebohm's father, Joseph Rowntree, and supported by money from the family's successful cocoa and chocolate business. Their aim stated in the Trust deed was to 'alleviate the evils which arise from the unsanitary and insufficient housing accommodation available for large numbers of the working class'.[1]

Raymond Unwin was commissioned to draw up plans for a new 'garden village', on land two miles from the centre of York, and he designed the homes with his partner Barry Parker. The aim was to build attractive houses with gardens, to house people from slum houses in York, not just Rowntree employees. The village is an expression of the garden city movement's architectural style, built at a density of 12 per acre, with front and back gardens, a school, shops and community centre – 'the Folk Hall'. The building was later extended to include a library and swimming pool, all being managed by the New Earswick Community Association.

The 30 houses in the first phase were built between 1898 and 1904, before the Trust was formally set up, and the second phase of 217 houses was built by 1919, without the benefit of any public subsidy. The 259 homes built in the inter-war years received subsidies under the Wheatley Housing Act.

Extensive modernisation was carried out to the earliest houses in the 1970s, including installing a bathroom, removing a bedroom and providing new cooking and heating appliances. The size of the back gardens was reduced in order to build new roads at the back of the houses, which made it possible to create safe pedestrian walkways between the front gardens. The trustees agonised long and hard about the plans, but in his history of New Earswick published in 1983, the Director of the Joseph Rowntree Foundation, Lewis Waddilove, wrote that the modernisation had been 'more fruitful than any of those concerned thought possible'.[2]

The rents were set as low as possible, so that they would be affordable by the poorest workers. Trustees had a strong concern that the new homes should be affordable to the lowest paid worker, while also seeking to reconcile this policy with their aim of making a reasonable return on the Trust's capital investment. Their reasoning was that, even though it was 'in no-one's personal interest, it was an object lesson to be followed by others'.

With the homes built over the past half century, New Earswick is now a village of over 1,000 homes. In its early years all the houses were built for rent, but there was a wide range of incomes among the tenants. By the 1980s the village was increasingly occupied by tenants earning low wages or dependent on welfare benefits. In order to preserve the original aim of creating a socially balanced community, the Trust decided to build some new homes for sale or shared ownership.

The first initiative was at Willow Bank in 1981 with low cost homes for sale, and this was followed by a shared ownership development at Woodlands Place in 1985. Three years later the Trust built a new mixed tenure development at Juniper Close, followed by the first flexible tenure project at Alder Way, where all purchasers could buy a 25 per cent, 50 per cent or 75 per cent stake, with the option of selling back to the Trust at any time in the future.

Since 1997 tenanted properties have been offered for sale to residents under the Government's voluntary purchase policy, with purchasers able to buy an equity stake through the Home-buy arrangement. In addition, the Trust makes some properties that became vacant available for sale on the open market, so as to sustain a balance of home ownership and rented houses.

What is striking about New Earswick is that there is no visible distinction of any kind between the rented and owner-occupied homes, which are integrated through every part of the village. The levels of satisfaction are extremely high, with 98 per cent of residents expressing satisfaction with their homes.

The Rowntree Housing Trust is now planning a new 540-home community on the edge of York, providing for a range of income groups and different tenures across the development. Four alternative master plans were commissioned, with extensive consultation with the local community to consider the different options. Separate studies have been carried out on the needs of children, young people and families; older people; and disabled people.

The houses are pepper-potted, mixed tenure homes, with 25 per cent for social renting and 10 per cent intermediate, probably Homebuy shared equity. The design will be chosen through an architectural competition, with an emphasis on high 'eco' standards of energy use and Lifetime Homes accessibility for every house, with additional wheelchair housing. There will be 20 acres of open space to include ponds, trees, wildlife habitat area, retained hedgerows, cycle routes and play areas for children. There will be a sustainable urban drainage system to pioneer good practice in water conservation.

Housing co-operatives in Liverpool

One of the striking, and surprising, features of housing in Liverpool is the presence of more than 50 housing co-operatives, set up by small groups of working class residents in the inner areas of the city as a route to escape from the run-down homes where they were living.

The first housing co-ops in Liverpool were formed in the Granby area in 1970 with the support of the Shelter Neighbourhood Action Project (SNAP). These co-ops started to buy and renovate street properties for their members; they also set up a new organisation, Neighbourhood Housing Services, to act as their architects.

Co-operative Development Services (CDS) was a small housing association set up in the Toxteth area of Liverpool in 1976. It had been formed by members with strong links to the wider co-operative movement and wanted to encourage local residents to play an active part in the control and management of their own homes. A year after it was formed CDS was approached by a small group of residents in a clearance area who had the dream of setting up a co-op so that they could actually have control of designing their own homes. The Weller Street Housing Co-operative became the first new-build housing co-op in the country where the members had control over the design of their future homes.

The epic struggle of the Weller Street co-op has been described in *The Weller Way*.[3] The book gives a vivid account of the co-op's relations with CDS, its architects, the City Council and the Housing Corporation, as well as the internal debates and disagreements within the co-op itself. As well as moments

The Holyland housing co-operative, Liverpool
Plus Housing Group

The Corn and Yates housing co-operative, Liverpool

Plus Housing Group

Hamlet village housing co-operative, Liverpool

Plus Housing Group

of celebration, there were also times of deep frustration and even despair. The outcome, however, was a group of new homes, in the heart of one of the most deprived neighbourhoods in the country, which are an inspiring achievement.

In the years from 1979 to 1983 fourteen more new-build co-ops were formed and followed the same route, ranging in size from 19 to 150 houses. Most of the co-ops were supported by CDS, who helped them to form their new organisations, acquire land from the council, secure funding from the Housing Corporation and commission architects to draw up their plans. For more than twenty years a key role was played by Catherine Meredith, the Director of CDS, whose personal belief in the benefits of resident control and the respect in which she was held by the City Council, Housing Corporation and other agencies was a very important factor in the development of so many co-ops.

From the 1980s it became difficult for new housing co-ops to follow the same route as the earlier Liverpool co-ops, as public funding priorities favoured established, large housing associations. However, new housing co-ops continued to be formed, including those set up for the elderly and several set up to house members from minority ethnic groups.

The best known of the housing co-ops is the Eldonian Housing Co-operative, which was set up by members of a close-knit community in the Vauxhall area, many descended from the Irish immigrants who settled in Liverpool in the 1840s. As a response to the City Council's plans to demolish the tenement flats where they were living and disperse the community to outlying estates, residents fought successive battles with the City Council and formed the Eldonian Community Association in 1978.

The first housing co-ops developed by the Eldonians were 100 homes in a refurbished walk-up block of flats and 130 homes built on five vacant sites. However, when the Labour Party gained control of the council in 1983 they took back the management of the properties, causing great anger in the local community. Despite this opposition the Eldonians persevered and eventually won support for building a new co-op of 145 homes on the site previously occupied by the Tate and Lyle sugar refinery, which had closed with a large loss of jobs in 1981, adding to the already severe unemployment problem. The co-op organised a competition on plans for the new housing, secured funding from the Housing Corporation and the future tenants were fully involved in the design process, so that no two houses are exactly the same.

A later phase of 150 homes was built on land reclaimed by the Merseyside Development Corporation and 15 flats and bungalows for the elderly have been built. The most recent development of 36 flats for older people was completed in 2004.

Coin Street housing co-operatives

For centuries the land across the river from the Houses of Parliament was undeveloped marshland, but as London's population soared in the nineteenth century low-paid workers crammed into the small houses built alongside the factories and wharves on the riverbank.

During the Second World War bombing destroyed many buildings and the site was chosen for the Festival of Britain in 1951. The National Theatre and National Film Theatre were built on the South Bank, alongside a number of large commercial buildings, but substantial parts of the area remained undeveloped. By the early 1970s the population had fallen from its pre-war peak of 50,000 to only 4,000.

In 1977 a developer put in a planning application to build Europe's largest hotel and in excess of one million square feet of office space on eight largely derelict sites at Coin Street in the heart of the South Bank area.

Local community organisations took the brave, but seemingly doomed, decision to oppose the developers, and submitted plans for their own alternative proposals, including affordable rented homes, local businesses and leisure activities. They put their case at two lengthy public inquiries, where developers who had initially put in competing bids joined forces, and, after the second inquiry, planning permission was granted for both the community group's and the developer's scheme.

The crucial turning point came when the Labour Party won the GLC election in 1981, Ken Livingstone was elected Leader of the Council and the GLC policy was changed from supporting the developer's scheme to backing the community group's proposals. The developers sold the parts of the site they owned to the GLC and in 1984 the whole site was sold to Coin Street Community Builders (CSCB) for £1 million.

Activists in the local community had already set up several local housing co-operatives for building and renovating housing which would enable low-paid residents to stay in the South Bank area, and when CSCB acquired the Coin Street sites it was decided to build housing co-ops, rather than conventional local authority or housing association homes.

The first housing co-op development (Mulberry) was completed in 1988, followed by Palm (1994), Redwood (1995) and Iroko (2001). In total they provide 220 high-quality affordable homes. Fifty per cent of new homes are let to people nominated by the local council, while the other 50 per cent are let to residents in the local community who are in housing need. As the leasehold is owned collectively by the housing co-operative, individual tenants do not have the right to own their homes and this has been critical in keeping the co-op properties as rented homes accessible to low-income residents.

New members are not expected to have any prior experience or knowledge of housing co-operatives, but every new member offered a home must complete a training programme of 11 three-hour sessions. These include not only information needed for running a co-operative, but also help to develop skills in communicating in meetings and making collective decisions.

A crucial strength of the CSCB lies in its ownership of the land. This has provided an asset base, which has grown in value with the development of the South Bank area, and enables it to borrow money for further new developments and also to put surpluses into community facilities.

Chestnut Avenue in 1972, New Earswick

Rowntree Housing Trust

Aerial view of the Walterton and Elgin estate, London

Philip Wolmuth

Consulting a resident on the Walterton and Elgin estate, London

Philip Wolmuth

Opening a newly converted home, on the Walterton and Elgin estate, London

Philip Wolmuth

The most ambitious of the projects carried out has been the redevelopment of the Oxo Tower Wharf, which includes a rooftop restaurant, a free viewing gallery, design studios, shops and 78 flats belonging to the Redwood Housing Co-op. It is an outstanding example of successful high quality, mixed-use development.

A major new development on the site adjoining the National Theatre is now being planned that will include a swimming pool and leisure centre and non-family affordable rented, shared equity and owner-occupied housing.

The transformation of the South Bank area over the past twenty years has been remarkable, visually, economically and socially. An area that had been disfigured by war damage and planning blight has been regenerated by community planning which has combined new commercial activities with good quality affordable housing and attractions for visitors to some of London's leading cultural events.

It is not difficult to imagine what the area would now be like if the plans for office development had been implemented. The skyline would be dominated by the high-rise building, the neighbourhood deserted after the office workers departed, the small number of homes occupied only by well-off residents or used as *pieds-à-terre* by business executives. The success of the community campaign has enabled it to develop as a successful neighbourhood where people from all walks of life and all areas of the world can live, work and play in a safe and peaceful environment.

Those achievements did not happen by chance, but only because a group of local residents had a vision for their local community. They refused to accept that they were powerless against the huge resources of the large private developers. They organised, campaigned and lobbied with great tenacity and astute tactical skills, using the media and attracting influential new supporters. When they suffered setbacks, as at times they did, they refused to concede defeat and prepared for yet another stage in the long campaign.

The best known of the Coin Street leaders is Iain Tuckett, who has been active since the Coin Street Action Group was formed in 1974, initially in setting up the first housing co-ops and drawing together the local residents to fight the office proposals, and for the past twenty years as Director of Community Street Builders. A crucial role has also been played by the small number of long-standing residents who shared in setting up the Action Group, and have played leading roles through all the different stages of the developments over the past thirty years.

CSCB is now a leading member of the growing network of social enterprises, which shows how organisations can combine entrepreneurial skills with strong social businesses, investing profits back into the local community rather than paying them out to absentee shareholders. Having demonstrated what can be achieved on the South Bank, it is in an exceptional position for inspiring that vision and sharing their experience and skills with others.

Walterton and Elgin Community Homes

Walterton and Elgin Community Homes (WECH) is a resident-controlled community organisation in north Paddington which won an epic battle to prevent Westminster City Council selling their homes and became the first organisation to use the 1988 Housing Act legislation to force the council to transfer the homes to the residents. In 1992 WECH took over the ownership and control of 921 homes from the council, and later received a 'dowry' of over £22 million to rehabilitate the properties.

The street properties were built between 1865 and 1885 and the London County Council bought the freehold in 1953. However, most of the leases were owned by private landlords, including the notorious Peter Rachman, who crammed the properties with tenants, charging high rents and carrying out few repairs. When the leases expired in 1964 the properties were in poor condition, with high levels of overcrowding and most homes lacking even basic amenities.

After the GLC had taken over responsibility from the LCC in 1965, it demolished one group of properties and built two tower blocks of 101 flats, Hermes and Chantry Points, and two low-rise blocks, Athens and Kincardine Gardens with 96 flats. The remaining properties were partly rehabilitated, for an estimated fifteen-year life. In 1985 both the flats and street properties were transferred to Westminster City Council as a result of the abolition of the GLC, and on acquiring the properties the council drew up a scheme to sell the properties without the knowledge of, or any consultation with, residents.

In response, the residents organised themselves into an Action Group and started a vigorous campaign to stop the homes being sold. They collected a petition signed by over 1,100 people and lobbied every meeting of the council's Housing Committee for more than three years. The council negotiated plans with developers for selling the estate, but the residents responded with surprise visits to the offices of the developers, including hiring a coach to transport members of the group. These trips were especially popular with older residents who enjoyed the unexpected bonus of a day out, but also took very seriously the opportunity they gave of confronting the developers who were seeking to take away their homes.

After several years of campaigning, the Action Group had still failed to persuade the council to drop their sales plan and demoralised tenants had started to move off the estate. When the 1988 Housing Act became law, however, the Action Group saw the opportunity it opened up for them to use the powers in the new legislation to force the council to sell the homes to a resident-controlled organisation. They sought advice from the locally based Paddington Churches Housing Association and the Housing Corporation, and were encouraged to form Walterton and Elgin Community Homes, which could claim the right to take over the estate. A committee was elected by the residents, including outside members with expertise in housing finance and management.

In April 1989 a coach load of residents from WECH delivered their formal application to buy the properties, but then a protracted battle followed over the valuation of the properties. The City Council argued that WECH should pay £1 million for the purchase. WECH argued that the amount of work needed to bring them to a satisfactory condition was so high that they had a negative value, and the council should pay WECH £63 million. Eventually the issue was referred to the District Valuer who ruled that the council should pay WECH £17.5 million. In order to increase the money available for renovation, WECH then succeeded in securing an extra £3.5 million from the Housing Corporation, in exchange for the council being able to nominate seventy tenants for re-housing in the modernised properties.

The transfer plan finally reached its critical stage. It would only go ahead if a majority of tenants voted in favour of the transfer to WECH in a secret ballot. The vote took place in 1992 and 72 per cent of eligible residents voted in favour, out of 82 per cent of residents who took part. It was a decisive victory for WECH's long campaign to ensure the residents should decide on the future of the homes.

However, the actual work of carrying out the renovation was only beginning. The architect chosen by WECH was Hilary Chambers, who had spent many years on renovation projects with London boroughs, and had recommended renovation of the Walterton estate when commissioned by the GLC in 1984. He had advised WECH when they were preparing their bid for taking over the estate, and was universally respected for his professional expertise and personal commitment to supporting the tenants.

During 1992 WECH embarked on an ambitious programme of consultation to enable residents to have as much choice as possible over the renovation of the home where they would be living. The architect explained the options for different layouts and an overall design brief was agreed for each of the dozen house-types, but each design could be modified to suit individual needs and wishes. Tenants were able to make choices over the kitchen units and layout, colours of tiles, bathroom fittings and front doors.

Housing officers visited every resident to discuss plans with them, and everything was done to meet as many of their wishes as possible. A guarantee was given that nobody would need to move against their wishes, and extra repairs were carried out for those tenants who wanted to stay in their existing home without all the disturbance which full-scale renovation would inevitably cause. A different kind of consultation programme was needed for residents in the blocks of low-rise flats. Most of the improvements were made with tenants staying in occupation, although some tenants in the smaller flats moved out while the work was done. Tenants were able to choose the type of kitchen unit, floor coverings, whether to have a bath or shower, types of windows and colours for decorations.

The most dramatic part of the building programme was the work on the two tower blocks, as they included no less than 20 miles of deadly sprayed asbestos and sprayed cement, and WECH had decided before taking over that there was no alternative to demolition. Tenants were re-housed from the flats before WECH took over, and exceptional measures were taken to ensure the safety of the building workers while carrying out the work. WECH appointed a specialist firm – Enviresponse – to monitor the process to make doubly sure that safety standards were maintained. Under pressure over the extent of asbestos in the flats, the council commissioned an independent report by a former local authority chief executive, John Barratt, that reached damning conclusions over the knowing neglect of safety standards:

> Despite the availability of the clearest advice, those acting on behalf of a public body took risks with the health of people who ought to have been entitled to assume that such risks were not being taken. It was abundantly clear that the bad conditions were known to decision-makers. But . . . the overriding objective of the Chairmen [of the council committees] was the defeat of the WECH bid. Surveys revealed a deplorable neglect of obvious asbestos-related dangers.[4]

The removal of the tower blocks made available land for WECH to build new homes, and there was extensive consultation over the plans and design of the new flats. The flats range from two to four storeys, with almost half having their own gardens. There was considerable debate over the number of new homes to be built, and eventually it was agreed to build 55 homes, compared with 202 flats in the tower blocks. There was a significant loss of dwellings, which WECH decided was justified to avoid building at too high a density for family housing. In line with WECH's policy, the flats were allocated to the future tenants a year in advance of completion, so that residents who were moving from within the estate could make choices over the way the conversion was carried out and on the fixtures and fittings chosen.

The extraordinary success of the WECH campaign owes a huge amount to the active involvement of residents, developed over many years. Three-quarters of the tenants and leaseholders are members, and WECH has given great importance to informing, consulting and encouraging active participation at every stage.

Jonathan Rosenberg, a resident on the estate who was a driving force in the campaign and then the co-ordinator of WECH during the development programme, played a key role. He showed extraordinary talent in finding tactics that outwitted the developers and the councillors, in attracting favourable publicity and in sustaining the active involvement of residents. He stresses that the high level of participation has only been achieved by a huge amount of hard work, knocking on doors to remind people of meetings, distributing reports to residents and consulting residents at every stage. A core of residents, such as Irene Blackman, have been stalwarts through every stage of the campaign.

What WECH has achieved is an outstandingly successful community campaign by local residents. They fought a long battle to defeat the council's plans to sell their homes to private developers, making an inspired use of the new housing legislation, and gave huge priority to involving residents in the programme for renovating and replacing the homes on the estate. Their report, *Against the Odds*,[5] recounts the WECH story, with a graphic account of every stage in the campaign, with many quotes from residents about the difference it has made to their lives, and also quotes from external 'experts' who have supported WECH through giving professional advice, as independent members of the Board and helping to secure positive publicity.

Astute tactics, professional expertise and imaginative leadership have all played important parts in WECH's achievements, but everything has been underpinned by a powerful conviction in the right of ordinary residents to control their own homes and the commitment to make that happen in the area of north Paddington where they live.

Conclusion

The examples of New Earswick, WECH and the Liverpool and Coin Street housing co-ops are very different, but what is common to all of them is the importance of their *vision*.

The story starts with the determination of Joseph and Seebohm Rowntree that people living in the overcrowded slums of York should be enabled to escape from those conditions, and their appointment of Raymond Unwin and Barry Parker to design a new settlement which combined the very best of sensitive design, use of open space and shared community amenities.

The people living in run-down inner city areas of Liverpool, and Waterloo and Paddington in London, also had a dream of renovating their existing homes or building new homes that reflected their choices of where and how they wanted to live. Buying the land and collectively owning the housing were crucial to their victories. Working with architects and other professionals who were committed to achieving the highest quality possible and empowering residents to make decisions were also critically important. Time and again in the stories of what happened, the words 'determination' and 'persistence' recur. The victories were not easily won. For all the excitement of spectacular victories, there were many times – cold winter evenings in long committee meetings and tramping the streets delivering leaflets and knocking on doors – when the campaign was not glamorous.

Walking round all of these neighbourhoods today is an inspiring and uplifting experience. In different styles they are well-designed, carefully planned homes, making imaginative use of individual and communal space. They look and feel like homes and neighbourhoods where people want to live, and are proud to live. Most contain a mix of owners and tenants, with some lease-holders and with shared equity, and there are no visible differences between any of the forms of tenure. In a range of ways too, the residents have been able to make choices, over the planning and design of their homes, the decisions on how they are managed and the communal facilities in their neighbourhood.

Chapter 13

Sharing housing wealth

In Chapter 6 it is estimated that the cost of implementing the programme for building new homes is £7 billion annually. It is difficult to estimate what the net capital cost will be of the programme of acquisitions and sales proposed in Chapter 8 for promoting socially mixed communities, but £2 billion a year for the next five years may be a reasonable assumption. The total cost of the proposals is therefore approximately £9 billion a year, compared to £3.5 billion planned expenditure on social housing investment in 2004/5. The net additional cost therefore is £5.5 billion a year. This chapter shows how the money for this can be obtained, including how it could be achieved by re-distributing resources within the current housing system.

The Government's spending plans for housing are now higher than over the past twenty years, although much less than the spending on housing was in the 1960s, when over 200,000 rented homes a year were built. Public spending on housing is not seen by the public as such a high priority as it was then, primarily because most people are reasonably well housed. There are fiercely competing demands for more public spending, with the greatest public support given to health care and education.

While the Labour Government has increased spending on public services substantially since 1997, projected future increases are much lower and many economic experts predict that increased taxation will be required to fund the planned spending programmes. In order to provide the money to fund the proposals put forward in this book, we need to look at new options.

The huge growth in owner occupation over the last fifty years has brought many benefits to people who have bought their homes – in better standards of housing, freedom to choose where they live and an increasingly valuable capital asset. Rising house prices have led to large windfall gains for most homeowners, especially in the last few years.

- The average value of the equity in each home is now £100,000. This excludes the value of any mortgage.
- Since 1980 the value of the equity in each home has increased fivefold in *real* terms, that is after allowing for the rate of inflation measured through the retail price index.

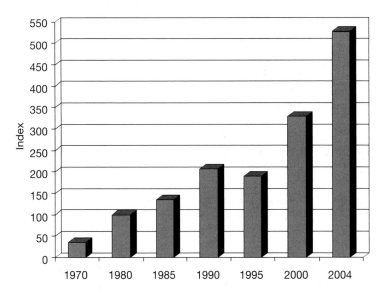

Graph 13.1 Growth in real value of housing assets (1970–2003)

The net equity of owner-occupied housing has grown from £36 billion in 1970 to £2,334 billion in 2004. Shown on an index where 1980 is 100, house prices have risen from 100 in 1980 to 524 in 2004, a fivefold increase (see Graph 13.1). On average, homeowners became over £20,000 wealthier in 2003 because of the increase in the value of their homes. Yet no tax is paid on these huge gains in personal wealth.

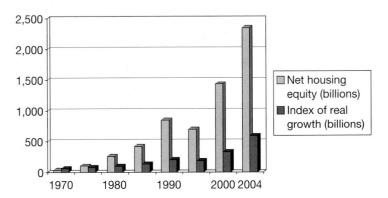

Graph 13.2 Growth in value of gross housing equity (1980 = 100)

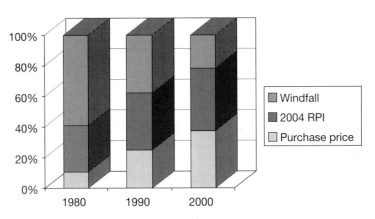

Graph 13.3 Value of windfall gains from home ownership

Most people remember very clearly how much they paid for each house they have bought, and how much they sold it for a number of years later. The growth in house prices is a subject of endless conversation and interest. Yet most people don't see the growth in the value of their home as a 'windfall gain' which might reasonably be taxed, as they expect to be taxed on income they earn.

The issue is highly emotive. The gains are not seen as being like real money in the bank. So long as an owner continues to live in the same home or sell in order to purchase a more expensive property, any gains may appear to be only notional. However, if they trade down or cease to own a property the increased value is realised as actual money. For many people who have owned their home it comprises the largest asset in their estate when they die, its value hugely swollen by the rise in house prices.

Table 13.1 shows examples of what has happened with rising house prices. The column 'RPI value' shows what the house would be worth if house prices had risen in line with the retail price index.

The table shows that homeowners are likely to have made 'windfall gains' averaging between £67,000 and £122,000 depending on whether they bought their home in 1980, 1990 or 2000. Yet unlike any money saved from their earnings this will not have been taxed at all. It is an untaxed windfall gain.

There is a curious attitude that has developed, which sees rising house prices as good news, in striking contrast to attitudes towards other form of inflation. This is because higher prices

Table 13.1 The windfall gains from home ownership

Date bought	Purchase price	RPI value 2004	Actual price 2004	Windfall gain
1980	£24,000	£67,000	£199,000	£122,000
1990	£63,000	£94,000	£190,000	£96,000
2000	£114,000	£125,000	£192,000	£67,000

benefit existing owners. What it ignores is the impact on people trying to buy a home for the first time, especially young people, who find it difficult or impossible to buy. It is also very unfair on the 30 per cent of the population who do not own a home and have no share in this wealth. They are completely left out of the property bonanza.

Taxing property can be a way of providing the resources to fund the proposals for housing investment put forward in this book. The exemption of housing from tax fuels the upward spiral of house prices and makes it harder for young people to buy their first home. Even modest rates of taxation on residential property would yield large sums, which could be used to finance spending on investment in social housing and more help for first time buyers. In order to tackle the housing shortage effectively, to halt the endlessly upward spiral of house prices and to reduce inequality in wealth such policies may be necessary.

Such changes are also very relevant to the reforms suggested in the Chancellor's assessment that as it currently operates the UK housing market is a major barrier to entry into the single currency. In particular the studies show that house prices are higher in the UK than in Germany and France, two of the most comparable economies, as a result of under-supply of housing in relation to demand and the very favourable tax treatment of home ownership, especially in relation to higher value properties.

In the past most measures of inequality and poverty have focused on differences of *income*. Yet it is also important to look at differences in the ownership of *assets*. The IPPR's work on 'asset-based welfare', for example, has shown that the most substantial inequalities in society are in wealth, especially between those who own shares, pensions and housing and those who rely solely on wages and/or benefits. The number of people with no assets at all has doubled over the past twenty years, from 5 per cent to 10 per cent. People who rent their homes are more likely to be among the asset-excluded, as they own no housing wealth.[1]

Capital gains tax

The most straightforward way of taxing windfall gains from the rise in house prices is through removing the exemption of the first home of owner-occupiers from Capital gains tax (CGT). This is a tax on the difference between the value of an asset when it is acquired and when it is sold. Any sum liable for CGT is included as taxable income within the annual tax assessment. At present any home occupied by the owner as his or her primary residence is exempt from CGT.

If this were to be levied immediately when a house is sold, and the proceeds used to purchase another, the argument against CGT is that it would discourage or prevent people moving home. This would be bad for labour mobility, as well as very unpopular. The way to avoid this is by allowing a 'roll over' of the tax when the receipts from selling are used for purchasing another property, only requiring the tax to be paid if there is no subsequent purchase or when the owner dies.

Table 13.2 is an estimate of the annual yield from CGT, assuming that 'roll over' were allowed.

There are strong arguments in support of taxing capital gains. It is a tax on unearned income, not earned income. It is broadly progressive because of being payable only by people who own assets. It is difficult to evade and cheap to administer, since revenue from CGT is incorporated within the overall income tax system. However, in the past any changes to CGT have not been applied retrospectively, but only to gains resulting after the date of the new rules being applied. The result of this would be

Table 13.2 Yields from capital gains tax

	1994/95	1995/96	1996/97	1997/98	1998/99	1999/00	2000/01	2001/02
Capital gains tax relief (£ million)	−340	−200	−240	−320	−560	1,200	1,320	2,400

Source: Steve Wilcox, *UK Housing Review*, 2004/5.

to exclude any revenue from past house price increases, and limit it to gains from future house price growth.

Inheritance tax

An alternative approach is to reduce the threshold for inheritance tax, and/or vary the rates of tax on different levels of asset. At present it is estimated that 40 per cent of legacies consists of the value of the homes owned by the deceased, and this share has been rising in line with the growth in housing prices. It is the primary reason why more estates are reaching or exceeding the current £275,000 threshold at which liability for inheritance tax starts.

Table 13.3 sets out what would be the yield from inheritance tax, if levied at a range of different rates. These show that very considerable sums could be raised, both from reducing the threshold at which estates are liable for tax and by imposing a higher rate than the present 40 per cent above the threshold. Thus if tax were charged on estates of over £150,000 at

Table 13.3 Yields from inheritance tax

Inheritance tax receipts (£ billion) by IHT threshold and rate for 2004–05 – rounded to nearest £100 million

Rates applied from April 2004	Tax rate (%)				
IHT threshold (£)	20	30	40	50	60
75,000	3.6	–	–	–	–
100,000	3.2	–	–	–	–
150,000	2.6	3.5	–	–	–
200,000	–	2.9	3.5	–	–
250,000	–	–	2.9	–	–
300,000	–	–	2.6	–	–
600,000	–	–	–	1.9	–
750,000	–	–	–	1.7	1.8
1,250,000	–	–	–	–	1.5

Source: Answer to Parliamentary Question asked by Karen Buck MP, Hansard, answered by Stephen Timms MP, 18 October 2004.

30 per cent, this would raise £3.5 billion a year. If tax were levied at 50 per cent on estates over £500,000 this would raise £1.9 billion. Neither of these would be draconian forms of taxation under any objective assessment, yet they would bring large sums of revenue which could be used to fund higher levels of housing investment.

As a general principle on taxation it is not sensible to tax unearned windfall gains less than earned income. What many people are now leaving in their wills are not the proceeds of a lifetime of hard work and thrift. They are the fortuitous gains from having owned a home in this country during a time when prices have risen far more rapidly than the general level of inflation.

Annual property tax

A third alternative approach is to levy an annual property tax on each privately owned dwelling. This is a policy which has long been advocated by John Muellbauer, an acknowledged expert on taxation issues and Professor of Economics at Oxford University. He set out the arguments for reform in an IPPR pamphlet published in 1990, *The Housing Disaster*. His views have been outlined most recently in a response to the analysis of the Barker Review, where he argues that a property tax has the merits of being progressive (i.e. the tax due rises as the value of the property increases); it would discourage under-use of properties, whether by being left empty or under-occupied; and it would act as an incentive to live in areas of lower housing demand and disincentive to live in high demand areas of the country.[2]

If a tax of 0.5 per cent were levied annually on the current market value of a residential property, this would yield £750 on an average priced house of £150,000. The total yield would be approximately £12 billion annually.

If such a property tax were introduced it would be possible to limit the tax levied on low-income owners, for example, by exempting properties with a value of under £50,000 and levying the tax at 0.25 per cent rate up to £100,000. It would also be possible to allow people to defer payment of a tax until the property is sold. This would be particularly helpful to the substantial number of older homeowners with low incomes. Obviously these measures would reduce the annual yield, especially in the early years after the tax was introduced.

There is a strong case for a property tax. It would raise substantial sums that could fund the proposed programme of housing investment. It would be a progressive tax, levying more on owners of valuable property, and with the possibility of reducing or deferring tax on low-income owners. It would not tax the windfall gains already accrued by existing owners, but in other respects it has many advantages.

One 'sweetener' for levying a property tax would be to reduce the level of stamp duty, which is a tax levied every time a dwelling is bought or sold. Stamp duty rates were increased four times between 1997 and 2000, with the rates of 3 per cent now applying to properties valued at over £250,000, and 4 per cent for properties valued at over £500,000. However, the minimum threshold for stamp duty was raised to £120,000 in the 2005 budget.

In addition the impact of stamp duty has increased as the result of rising house prices: the yield from transactions on residential dwellings rose from £1.7 billion in 1998/9 to £3.6 billion in 2002/3.

In his article on 'Taxation Issues' in the 2004/5 issue of the *UK Housing Review*, Steve Wilcox argues that there is a strong case for reforming stamp duty, on a number of grounds:

> The 'slab' structure of the duty rates, which are applied to the full value of the property, rather than to the marginal element of value above each threshold, leads to artificial bunching of prices just below each threshold level. It also encourages avoidance measures such as inflated payments for 'fixtures and fittings' so that the declared purchase price remains just below threshold levels.
>
> It can also be argued to be a tax on mobility, as it is only paid by homeowners when they move. If you move twice in

ten years you pay more than the household, in equivalent value property, that moves only once in that period. If, however, stamp duty was levied on the basis of capital gains, rather than total values, the tax raised would be the same for both households, regardless of how frequently they moved.[3]

If a property tax were introduced, its impact could be alleviated by either reducing stamp duty to a much lower rate, say a flat rate of 1 per cent on all transactions, or possibly by abolishing it altogether.

The major difficulty about introducing a property tax is that it would be seen as duplicating council tax. Although the purpose of council tax is to provide revenue for local authority spending, it is levied in tax bands on the value of individual properties. In order to resolve this problem Muellbauer proposes replacing council tax by a local income tax. However, in its recent review of local authority finance the Government rejected radical reforms of this kind in favour of more limited changes to the current system.

A land tax

A still more far-reaching option is a tax on the ownership of land, as recently proposed by Iain McLean, Professor of Politics at Oxford University.[4] There is a long history of land tax being advocated by socialist and progressive reformers. The best-known proponent of a land tax was Henry George, who set out his arguments in his book *Progress and Poverty* in 1879, having developed his ideas as a journalist in San Francisco reporting on the huge profits accumulated from the Gold Rush. David Lloyd George proposed a tax on land values in his famous radical budgets as Liberal Chancellor of the Exchequer in 1909, and again in 1914, but his proposals were not implemented due to the outbreak of war.

The 1947 Town and Country Planning Act included provisions for a 'betterment tax' levied on the increases in the value of land resulting from the granting of planning permission, especially when this changed the way in which land could be used. However, this part of the Act was short-lived as the Conservative Government repealed it in 1951. Subsequent plans for taxing land by Labour Governments in 1967 and 1974 were dropped for fear of proposals for carrying out new development being withheld or postponed. The most recent official assessment of the case for taxing land was in the Barker Review (see Chapters 2 and 6), which recognised that there was a strong economic argument for taxing increases in land values resulting from planning permission being given, but concluded that in practice it was unfeasible.[5] McLean challenges this conclusion by arguing that a land tax should be based on the capital value, not on transactions. Thus the value of the land 'would not depend on whether (it) had planning permission, but on whether the market believed it would get planning permission'.[6]

Housing Bonds

Asset-based welfare starts from the premise that ownership of assets can positively affect an individual's well-being and lead to wider social and economic benefits. The IPPR report, *The Asset Effect*,[7] cites research findings showing that the holding of assets leads to a wide range of benefits over time, including improved educational attainment, better labour market performance and improved health.

The losers in the growth of housing wealth are tenants. They have no stake in the rising value of the equity of the homes where they live. The different experience of owners and tenant is the single greatest cause of the widening equity divide.

To date, ideas for enabling tenants to have an equity stake have focused on extending home ownership. Shared ownership is being promoted by the Government as a way of enabling people to own a share in the equity of their home, as well as a way of providing affordable housing for people who cannot afford full home ownership.

A new approach to helping tenants to accumulate assets has been proposed by Rachel Terry in a report published by the

Chartered Institute of Housing (CIH) and Shelter.[8] It is designed to give new choices for people who cannot currently become homeowners, or do not wish to take on the responsibilities that come with home ownership.

The HomeSave scheme has three main elements:

1   A savings scheme through which tenants receive an initial deposit for opening a Flexible Savings Account, and their savings are matched £1 for £1 by their landlord up to a suggested limit of £250. It is proposed that the landlord's contribution will be reimbursed by the Government.
2   Tenants with a minimum of £200 in the savings account will be able to open a Housing Investment Account, to build up an investment in affordable rented housing. Properties purchased through this scheme will be part-funded by an interest-free equity loan from the housing association managing the property representing 25 per cent of its value.
3   A Shared Ownership Scheme for tenants who have saved the difference between their monthly rent and the monthly shared ownership costs in the Housing Savings or Investment Account will enable them to acquire a share in the equity of their home.

The CIH and Shelter have suggested that the scheme could be piloted by different social landlords, and are seeking support from the Government for the proposals. It fits well with the growing political interest in policies that would tackle financial exclusion, promote a stronger savings culture among low-income tenants and provide new options for investment in housing for people who cannot afford to own.

An alternative approach is to give tenants a rebate on the rents they have paid through giving them a Housing Bond. This scheme could apply to all tenants, including private tenants, or be limited to tenants of local authorities and housing associations. As an example of how it would work, where a tenant has paid the full rent due in a year, he/she should receive a Housing Bond valued at £1,000. This could be cashed at their monetary value, but if retained as a Bond would be re-valued each year in line with the average growth in house prices.

One option is not to give Housing Bonds to people on full housing benefit, on the grounds that they have not paid the rent from income that they have earned. However, tenants receiving part housing benefit would be entitled to a reduced value Housing Bond, on a sliding scale. Any rent arrears outstanding at the end of the year would be deducted from the value of the Housing Bond. An alternative option is to include all tenants, or at least people over retirement age and people with disabilities, on the grounds that those on full housing benefit are most likely to be people without any assets.

If the tenant decides to buy a property on the open market, any Housing Bond(s) could be cashed at their housing price growth value. However a tenant exercising the right to buy should not benefit from both an RTB discount and a Housing Bond.

The cost of Housing Bonds could be met through a direct payment from the Government and channelled through the social landlord. For tenants of social landlords an alternative would be to pay for the Bond through a charge against the equity of the property occupied by the tenant, which would have the advantage that it would not count as additional public spending. For the landlord this would reduce the equity value of their property. Inevitably the implications of this on the overall financial health of the landlord would vary considerably between different social landlords, and would be a factor that the Government and Housing Corporation would need to take into account in giving loan approvals and housing subsidies.

Creating Housing Bonds would enable tenants to build up ownership of capital assets in a similar way to homeowners, even if on a smaller scale. Bonds could be used to help in house purchase, but also as a capital asset in other ways. Where a tenant dies, the value of the Housing Bond could be passed on to any successor tenant or cashed to contribute to the value of their estate.

Taxing housing wealth

The proposals for taxing windfall gains by capital gains tax, inheritance tax and a property tax are in line with the measures needed for increasing housing supply identified in the Barker Review and also in the study for the Chancellor's five economic assessments. In addition to the other benefits, they would also have the effect of leading to lower house prices and greater stability in the housing market.

They would also encourage a less wasteful acquisition of housing assets. At present there is an incentive for buyers to purchase the largest property they can afford, in order to enhance their gains from future increases in its value. In some instances, especially in areas of high house price inflation, people acquire properties without any intention of occupying or letting them but simply to benefit from untaxed capital gains. Such behaviour leads to an extremely inefficient use of scarce housing space, and is a moral affront in a society where a large number of people still lack a proper home.

The proposals for changing stamp duty would reduce revenue from taxation, but could be included within a wider package of changes, such as the introduction of a property tax. It is better to levy tax on the actual ownership of assets rather than on the act of buying them, which can be a disincentive to mobility.

The proposals for a Housing Bond for tenants would require extra public spending but this is justified in order to reduce the asset inequality between homeowners and tenants.

Through a combination of the different policy options discussed in this chapter, it would be possible to raise the additional resources needed for the proposed spending and narrow the wealth gap by enabling tenants to build up a capital asset.

It would be possible to make changes to inheritance tax and capital gains tax immediately. The introduction of a property tax could only be made as part of wider changes, since it would not be feasible to levy both an annual property tax alongside the current council tax.

Proposals for taxing land should be given further study, including a consideration of the case for reintroducing some form of betterment levy, an evaluation of the current arrangements for securing social benefits through Section 106 agreements, and the more far-reaching proposals for an annual tax on the value of land.

Inevitably any proposals for taxing housing wealth will be controversial. For example, opinion surveys have shown strong hostility to even the present levels of inheritance tax, and any proposal for reducing the threshold of liability for tax would be likely to arouse vehement opposition.

This chapter has focused primarily on ways of raising tax revenue from the ownership of property and land. An alternative is to increase taxes on income, especially the huge incomes received by the growing number of extremely wealthy people. There is the need for a more informed public discussion of the options, but ultimately it is for the Government to make decisions in its Budget on how revenue is raised to meet plans for public spending. The key conclusion from this book, however, is simple: current plans for public spending on housing investment are far too low. An estimated extra £5.5 billion a year is needed, by whichever means of raising more resources are chosen.

There will be opposition to plans for higher taxation, but this can be countered by a public campaign that puts forward the benefits. At present, existing owners benefit from house price inflation, while aspiring purchasers suffer. Using the proceeds of taxing property to help first time buyers would in effect re-cycle a part of the wealth of current owners to help the next generation gain access to home ownership. The rate of house price growth would be reduced, so as to make home ownership more affordable. Tax revenue would be increased so as to fund a much larger programme of affordable housing, for both homes to rent and lower cost home ownership, and could also be used to enable tenants to build up capital assets.

A package of measures is possible that would re-distribute resources, including within the housing system, in order to achieve key policy objectives. They would be fiscally progressive; reduce or remove the current undesirable tax on housing mobility; and reduce the inequality between owners and tenants in ownership of capital assets. Most importantly they would make it possible to reduce the unacceptable levels of overcrowding and homelessness, build the number of new homes that are needed, achieve the regeneration of deprived neighbourhoods and develop many more socially inclusive, mixed tenure communities.

Chapter 14

A new vision for the future

An important theme of this book is the importance of learning from history and understanding the reasons for the changes in housing policy and tenure that have taken place. They are shaped by the interplay of many different factors, including economic, social and political developments as well as changes in household patterns and aspirations.

The most significant tenure change during the last century was the growth of home ownership, rising from 10 per cent of households owning their home in 1914 to 70 per cent in 2000. It is a tenure that enables people to have choice over where they live and a sense of pride and control over their home. However the *way* in which it has developed has increased social polarisation and inequality.

The expanding suburbs provided a route out of crowded inner cities for many people buying their own home. However, while some new council homes were built in the suburbs there were many more examples of resistance to building local authority housing outside the urban heartlands. The prejudice against council tenants was shown at its most dramatic in the building of the Cutteslowe wall in Oxford, a physical symbol of class prejudice and social exclusion, but also in many less visible forms of resistance to building public housing in suburban or rural communities.

The pioneers of council housing in the early twentieth century aimed to build well-designed homes in self-contained and socially mixed communities. Those designed by Raymond Unwin reflected key ideas from the garden city movement and the arts and crafts tradition, and the Tudor Walters Committee translated these into practical advice for developing good quality homes. They were built to standards equal to, and in some instances better than, new private housing.

As the Minister responsible for housing in the post-war Labour Government, Nye Bevan also had a vision of council housing providing homes for people from all walks of life. In the immediate post-war years local authorities built more than three quarters of all new homes, all with higher space standards. Bevan was insistent that 'we will be judged in twenty years not by the number of new homes but by the quality of the homes we have built'.[1]

Housing priorities changed sharply with the new Conservative Government. The growth of home ownership was encouraged under the slogan of 'a property owning democracy'. The growth of the suburbs in the inter-war years had shown the strength of the aspirations of the growing middle class to own their homes and in the 1950s the expansion resumed with the high levels of employment and rising post-war affluence.

Owning your home has many advantages for those who can afford it, and the level of home ownership has increased with rising incomes in almost every industrialised society. In Britain, however, the growth of home ownership has been fuelled by a succession of financial incentives, notably mortgage tax relief and generous discounts on the right to buy. It has also been encouraged by a political ideology, which has promoted home ownership as inherently superior to renting.

The abolition of Schedule A tax in the 1961 Budget, ending the tax on the notional benefit that owner-occupiers enjoyed from occupying their home rent free while retaining tax relief on mortgage interest payments, is now an almost forgotten fiscal change, and one unknown to most people aged under 60. At the time, however, it was an important as well as symbolic tax reform that reflected the preferential attitude of the Government towards homeowners.

Meanwhile, council housing was suffering a series of damaging body blows. As urban local authorities experienced resistance from politicians and local residents when seeking to build new homes in suburban and rural areas they were forced to build homes only within their own boundaries, at higher densities and frequently on less desirable sites. Their inability to access land outside their own areas was one important, although largely unrecognised, factor which pushed them into the disastrous policy of building large estates of systems-built housing.

From the 1970s onwards the social make-up of council housing changed dramatically, with a marked increase in the number of low-income tenants. By the 1990s fewer than half of households renting from local authorities had a member working, and the majority were at least partly dependent on welfare benefits.

This change is usually portrayed as wholly undesirable, the so-called 'residualisation' of council housing. In fact the opening up of council housing to more of the poorest households was a desirable and overdue change. As Chapter 1 showed, the rents of the early council homes, and also housing trust properties, had been too high for most unskilled and low-waged workers. Members of the skilled working class predominantly occupied council housing.

During the 1970s many local authorities reformed their allocation policies to give priority to applicants in severe housing need, especially in response to the recommendations of the influential Cullingworth Report. The 1972 Housing Finance Act led to a statutory rent rebate scheme that, for the first time, enabled the poorest wage earners to afford council rents. The 1977 Homeless Persons Act placed a duty on local authorities to secure accommodation for homeless households in priority need. Many of these were one-parent families on low incomes and other poorer families who had not been able to obtain council housing.

The housing of more low-income tenants would not have been a problem if council homes had been integrated within neighbourhoods of owner-occupied and privately rented housing. It became a serious problem because single tenure estates housed only low income, predominantly non-earning tenants, and so created neighbourhoods of concentrated poverty.

A recurring theme of this book has been to argue that social housing should not be equated with council housing estates. A range of policies to re-shape the geography of social housing, and proposals for achieving this have been set out in the chapters on increasing choice and promoting socially mixed communities.

The chapter on Liverpool has shown that the surplus supply of housing makes it possible to increase home ownership in the city while still retaining an adequate supply of rented accommodation. By contrast, as a result of the high value of the equity in their existing accommodation, there is the potential for enabling tenants living in flats in inner London to have a choice of moving out, especially families who are overcrowded and others dissatisfied with their existing accommodation.

This opens up opportunities to increase the provision of socially rented homes in outer London suburbs, as well as possibilities for people to move to market towns, seaside resorts and commuter suburbs. It can be a way of opening up a new dimension to policies for choice-based lettings, where the opportunities are not limited to the existing stock of socially rented housing, but are extended to existing or newly built private housing providing this can be acquired at prices not greater than the value of the accommodation currently occupied.

There is a growing consensus that new housing developments should contain a mix of tenures, preferably without any spatial separation or physical differences. Programmes for the regeneration of housing estates increasingly include diversification of tenure, especially to provide homes for sale within estates that previously contained only rented housing.

What has been ignored to date is the potential for radically changing the physical location of socially rented housing by a major programme of acquisitions and sales. Excluding vacancies resulting from transfers, over 100,000 existing socially rented dwellings become vacant each year. When this happens there is the option of selling these properties and using the proceeds to purchase different ones in order to diversify the portfolio and produce a more balanced mix of properties. In practice, managing such a process may be a complex operation, involving balancing the proceeds and costs from different property transactions, so as to achieve the future property portfolio that best matches housing needs and aspirations.

Changes in the role of the state

A critical issue in housing policy has been the role that the state should play in the provision of housing. The nineteenth century was the heyday of *laissez faire* economics, and the dominant political parties were resistant to increasing the role of the state in tackling poor housing and poverty. Legislation was only enacted when the slums were recognised as a danger to the health of the whole population, including wealthier residents as well as the impoverished families living in the overcrowded tenements.

The pressure for state action grew towards the turn of the century, but the decisive change in political attitudes came at the end of the First World War. While the immediate impetus was fear of insurrection, the underlying factor was the extension of the voting franchise and the greater political power of the working class who rejected reliance on free market forces to provide better quality, affordable homes.

From 1919 until 1979 successive governments, of different political colours, entrusted local authorities with the leading direct role in housing provision, both to replace the old Victorian slums and to build new homes for the growing number of households. The new housing was subsidised to make rents affordable to most working class tenants, although in many areas the rents were still too high for the lowest paid.

The 1974 Housing Act marked a new turning point, enabling registered housing associations to provide subsidised homes. While the Labour Party saw the role of housing associations as complementing direct local authority provision, the Conservative Party increasingly saw housing associations as replacing directly owned and managed council housing.

A range of developments in recent years seems to be leading to a more complex pattern of relationships. For most of the twentieth century, housing provision was dominated by two distinct forms of housing, owner occupation and social renting, with the private rented sector experiencing a long decline until it reached a plateau at the end of the 1980s. At the top of the hierarchy has been owner occupation: the tenure of choice for people who could afford it, well-funded by specialist mortgage lenders, and subsidised by mortgage tax relief and other tax exemptions.

Next in the hierarchy came council housing. Through the middle years of the century it was the tenure occupied by a large number of working class households, directly provided and managed by local authorities, directly subsidised by central government, but losing popularity. By the closing years of the century, however, council housing lost its place in the hierarchy to housing association provision, increasingly favoured by successive governments, well-subsidised by central government, and chosen by tenants as their new landlord in almost half of all local authority areas. However, in 2004 there were still over two million tenants renting their homes from local authorities, and the new breed of Arm's Length Management Organisations (ALMOs) opened up a new option for well-performing local authority housing departments and their tenants.

In recent years it has become fashionable to predict the total demise of council housing, but such a verdict now seems premature at least. A number of the best-performing housing authorities have set up ALMOs and been rewarded with extra funding for investment, which enables them to retain municipal ownership of their housing stock while transferring management responsibility to an arm's length organisation.

The aim for the future should be to have a range of tenures, of equal status and esteem, providing for different housing needs and aspirations, with people able to have as much choice as possible over where they live. While most households will want to own their home, shared equity will be a valuable option for people who cannot afford the full cost of ownership. Socially rented housing will be provided by a range of land-lords, including local authorities directly managing housing, ALMOs and different types of registered social landlords (RSLs).

A new policy programme

A major purpose of this book is to challenge the belief that little can be done to reverse the growth of inequality and social polar-isation. It has shown that there are new solutions, which are practical and can make a real difference.

The key challenge is to develop housing policies that learn from past mistakes and set out plans for homes and commun-ities in the twenty-first century. The vision should be to provide sufficient good quality homes for all, where people live in socially balanced neighbourhoods that reflect the diversity of society, and where people in all tenures have choice over where they live. The most urgent task is to reduce the unacceptable number of homeless households in temporary accommodation and families experiencing severe overcrowding.

New policies are needed to widen the opportunities for more people to have choice over where they live, to develop more socially mixed communities and to enable tenants to share in the benefits from owning capital assets. This book makes the case for five major priorities:

1 Building 300,000 homes a year, with at least 90,000 for people who cannot afford to buy.
2 Ending the use of temporary accommodation for homeless families and making it unnecessary for anyone to become homeless.
3 Promoting inclusive communities by creating an integrated mix of tenures and incomes across all types of neighbour-hood.

4   Giving tenants more choice through the expansion of choice-based lettings and by buying vacant properties chosen by tenants.
5   Creating a Housing Bond for tenants, which will enable them to build up capital assets and will narrow the wealth divide between owners and tenants.

If the case for these proposals is accepted the key question is how the money will be raised to pay for them. While public spending on housing investment has been increased in successive Spending Reviews since 2000 the scale of spending still falls significantly short of what is required.

The policies put forward in Chapter 13 show how the increase in funding could be provided by changes to inheritance tax or capital gains tax designed to recycle the very large windfall gains that have increased the assets owned by existing homeowners. There are strong arguments on grounds of equity and social justice for taxing this unearned growth in housing wealth. However, the evidence from polling data and analysis of public opinion shows that such taxes would be very unpopular with those who would pay them. It may be that a more acceptable way would be simply to increase taxes on income, either directly or indirectly.

What is not acceptable is to do nothing. Current policies will not achieve satisfactory housing for all members of the community, especially those who are severely overcrowded or in temporary accommodation because they are homeless. They will not ensure that there is an adequate supply of affordable housing in areas of greatest housing demand, including for essential public service workers. They will not make it possible to end concentrations of poverty in deprived social housing estates. This can only be achieved by a radical reshaping of the geography of housing tenure in order to provide socially diverse and balanced communities in these types of area.

The key question, which is critical to attitudes to poverty and inequality in a rich industrialised society like Britain, is whether political leadership will be shown in advancing such policies, and whether sufficient public support can be secured from the better-off citizens who will be asked to pay higher taxes. Achieving it will not be easy, but it is far better than doing nothing.

Notes

Chapter 1: Homes fit for heroes

1 There were numerous books written describing housing conditions in the nineteenth century, including Friedrich Engels, *The Condition of the Working Class in England in 1844* (1892), Henry Mayhew, *London Labour and the Working Poor* (1851), James Hole, *The Home of the Working Class* (1985 [1866]), in addition to those referred to directly in the text.

2 Edwin Chadwick, *Report on the Condition of the Labouring Poor*, 1842.

3 Edith Gaudie, *Cruel Habitations*, 1974.

4 Andrew Mearns, *The Bitter Cry of Outcast London*, 1883.

5 Octavia Hill, *Homes of the London Poor*, 1883.

6 Anne Power, *Property before People*, 1987.

7 John Burnett, *A Social History of Housing 1815–1970*, 1978.

8 Gareth Stedman Jones, *Outcast London*, 1971.

9 Earl of Derby, speech in Liverpool, June 1871, printed in T. H. Sanderson (ed.) *Speeches and Addresses*, 1894

10 Raymond Unwin, *Nothing Gained by Overcrowding*, 1912.

11 Burnett, op. cit.

12 Walter Long, President of the Local Government Board, quoted in Richard Reiss, *The Home I Want*, 1918.

13 Seebohm Rowntree, memorandum for Housing Panel in England and Wales of the Ministry of Reconstruction, 1917.

14 Paul Barton Johnson, *Land Fit for Heroes, the Planning of British Reconstruction, 1916–1919*, 1968.

15 Barton Johnson, op. cit.

16 Barton Johnson, op. cit.

17 Burnett, op. cit.

18 Peter Collison, *The Cutteslowe Wall*, 1963. Among the active opponents of the wall were Richard Crossman, then an Oxford Labour Councillor, and Sir Stafford Cripps, who was the barrister representing the City Council in their legal action seeking to dismantle the wall.
19 Labour Party, *Let's Face the Future*, 1945.
20 Michael, Foot, *Aneurin Bevan* 1973.
21 Michael, Foot, op. cit.
22 Patrick Abercrombie, *Greater London Plan*, 1945.
23 Report of Reith Committee on New Towns.
24 Peter Hennessy, *Never Again*, 1992.
25 Kenneth Morgan, *Labour in Power 1945–51*, 1984.
26 Steve Hilditch, personal communication with author.

Chapter 2: The rise of home ownership

1 Harold Macmillan, *Tides of Fortune*, 1969.
2 Peter Hall, *The Containment of Urban England*, 1973.
3 J. S. Millar, *Manchester City Region, Review and Prospects*, 1968, quoted in Peter Hall, *The Containment of Urban England*, 1973.
4 Peter Hall, op cit.
5 Ken Young, and John Kramer, *Strategy and Conflict in Metropolitan Housing*, 1978.
6 Kate Barker, *Review of Housing Supply*, interim report, 2003.

Chapter 3: The mass housing disaster

1 Patrick Dunleavy, *Politics of Mass Housing*, 1981.
2 Dunleavy, op. cit.
3 Dunleavy, op. cit.
4 Alison Ravetz, *Council Housing and Culture*, 2000.
5 Raphael Samuel, *New Left Review*, 1962.
6 Jerry White, *London in the Twentieth Century*, 2001.
7 Dunleavy, op. cit.
8 Anne Power, *Estates on the Edge*, 1997.

Chapter 4: The changing nature of rented housing

1 Edith Gaudie, *Cruel Habitations*, 1974.
2 Seebohm Rowntree, *Poverty: a Study in Town Life*, 1901.
3 Margery Spring Rice, *Working Class Wives*, 1938, quoted in Sheila Rowbotham, *Hidden from History*, 1973.
4 Rice, op. cit.

5 Alan Holmans, 'The context for housing policy since 1975, statistical time series with commentary', 2005.
6 Central Housing Advisory Committee, *Council Housing: Purposes, Procedures and Priorities*, 1969.
7 Holmans, op. cit.
8 Holmans, op. cit.
9 Roger Burrows, *Unpopular Places: Area Disadvantage and Geography of Misery in England*, 1998.
10 Social Exclusion Unit, *Strategy for Neighbourhood Renewal*, 1998.
11 Holmans, op. cit.
12 Mark Stephens, Nicky Burns and Lisa Mackay, *Social Market or Safety Net*, 2002.

Chapter 5: Managing social housing

1 Chris Holmes, *The Other Notting Hill*, 2005.
2 Association for Public Service Excellence, *Housing Options*, 2003.
3 Hal Pawson and Cathie Fancy, *Maturing Assets*, 2003.
4 Pawson and Fancy, op. cit.
5 David Page, *Building for Communities: a Study of New Housing Association Estates*, 1993.

Chapter 6: Building sustainable communities

1 Social Exclusion Unit, *A New Commitment to Neighbourhood Renewal*, 2000.
2 Kate Barker, *Review of Housing Supply*, final report, 2004.
3 Julie Foley, *The Problems of Success*, 2004.
4 Alan Holmans, Sarah Mark and Christine Whitehead, *Building for the Future*, 2004.
5 CABE, *Assessing the Design Quality of New Homes*, 2004.
6 CABE, *Shaping Future Homes*, 2004.

Chapter 8: Creating socially mixed communities

1 Tudor Walters Committee, 1918.
2 Aneurin Bevan, House of Commons, 1949.
3 Page and Boughton, *Housing Today*, 1998.
4 IPPR, *Forum for Social Housing*, 2000.
5 IPPR, op. cit.
6 Gillian Tindall, *The Fields Beneath*, 1977.
7 North Islington Housing Rights Project, *Street by Street*, 1974.

8 St Mungo's Annual Report, 2004.
9 Alan Berube, *Mixed Communities in England*, 2005.

Chapter 9: Widening choice

1 MORI poll for CABE, 2002.
2 Housing Green Paper, *Quality and Choice*, 2000.
3 Bradford City Council, 2003.
4 Ridgehill Housing Association, Annual report, 2002.

Chapter 10: Liverpool: a city reborn

1 Liverpool: Port, Docks and City, *Illustrated London News*, 1886.
2 Edwin Chadwick, *Report on the Condition of the Labouring Poor*, 1842.
3 Mike Fletcher, *The Making of Liverpool*, 2004.
4 Lord Gifford, Wally Brown and Ruth Bundey, *Loosen the Shackles*, 1989.
5 Brendon Nevin, Peter Lee, Lisa Goodson, Alan Murie and Jenny Phillimore, *Changing Housing Markets and Urban Regeneration in the M62 Corridor*, 2001.
6 Plus Housing Group Annual Report, 2003/4.

Chapter 11: London: a world city

1 Ken Young and John Kramer, *Strategy and Conflict in Metropolitan Housing*, 1978.
2 Ken Young and Pat Garside, *Metropolitan London: Politics and Urban Change*, 1982.
3 Young and Kramer, op. cit.
4 Jerry White, *London in the Twentieth Century*, 2001.
5 Interviews with constituents by Karen Buck MP, 2004.
6 Greater London Authority, *Towards a London Plan*, 2000.
7 Greater London Authority, *Homes for a World City*, 2000.
8 Greater London Authority, *Draft London Plan*, 2002.
9 Greater London Authority, *Draft London Plan, Panel Report*, 2003.
10 Prime Minister's Strategy Unit, *London Analytical Report*, 2003.
11 Prime Minister's Strategy Unit, *London Project Report*, 2004.
12 London Housing Board Task Force, *Sustainable Communities: Mobility and Choice*, 2004.
13 London Housing Board, *Capital Homes: The London Housing Strategy, 2005–2016*, 2005.

14 Greater London Authority, *Housing Capacity Study*, 2005.
15 Greater London Authority, *London Household Survey*, 2003.

Chapter 12: Oases of excellence

1 Rowntree trust deed, 1902.
2 Lewis Waddilove, *New Earswick*, 1983.
3 Alan McDonald, *The Weller Way*, 1986.
4 John Barratt, *Report on Westminster City Council's Management of Hermes and Chantry Points*, 1996.
5 Walterton and Elgin Community Homes, *Against the Odds*, 1998.

Chapter 13: Sharing housing wealth

1 Dominic Maxwell, IPPR report, *Fair Dues*, proposed restructuring inheritance tax to make it more progressive. Under these proposals it would be levied at 20 per cent on assets above the threshold up to £200,000, rising to 50 per cent on assets worth over £800,000. It was estimated that the net result would be an extra £160 million a year in tax revenue. The proposals are presented in the report as reforms designed to tackle inequality, with the proceeds from extra income used to fund an increase in baby bonds. However, they leave the threshold of inheritance tax at its current level of £275,000, with no tax on any estates below that value. At present this would leave over 90 per cent of estates not liable for any tax, despite many now containing a substantial element due to the windfall gains from home ownership.
2 John Muellbauer, *Property and Land, Taxation and the Economy after the Barker Review*, 2004.
3 Steve Wilcox, *UK Housing Review, 2004/5*.
4 Iain McLean, 'Land tax: options for reform', in paper for IPPR/Oxford seminar on 'New Politics of Ownership', 2004.
5 Kate Barker, *Review of Housing Supply*, final report, 2004.
6 McLean, op. cit.
7 Paxton and Wynner, *The Asset Effect*, 2001.
8 Rachel Terry, *HomeSave*, 2005.

Chapter 14: A new vision for the future

1 Nye Bevan, quoted in Michael Foot, *Aneurin Bevan*, 1973.

Bibliography

Abercrombie, Patrick (1945), *Greater London Plan*, Standing Conference on London and South East Regional Planning.

Association for Public Service Excellence (2003), *Housing Options*, Manchester, APSE.

Association of London Government (2004), *Overcrowding in London*, London, Association of London Government.

Barker, Kate (2003), *Review of Housing Supply*, interim report, London, HM Treasury.

Barker, Kate (2004), *Review of Housing Supply*, final report, London, HM Treasury.

Barratt, John (1996), *Report on Westminster City Council's Management of Hermes and Chantry Points*, Westminster City Council.

Barton Johnson, Paul (1968), *Land Fit for Heroes, the Planning of British Reconstruction, 1916–1919*, Chicago and London, Chicago University Press.

Berube, Alan (2005) *Mixed Communities in England: a US Perspective on Evidence and Policy Prospects*, York, Jospeh Rowntree Foundation.

Burnett, John (1978), *A Social History of Housing 1815–1970*, London, Methuen.

Burrows, Roger (1998), *Unpopular Places: Area Disadvantage and Geography of Misery in England*, York, Joseph Rowntree Foundation.

CABE (2004), *Assessing the Design Quality of New Homes*, London CABE.

CABE (2004), *Shaping Future Homes*, London, CABE.

Central Housing Advisory Committee (1969), *Council Housing: Purposes, Procedures and Priorities*, London, HMSO.

Chadwick, Edwin (1842), *Report on the Condition of the Labouring Poor*, London, Poor Law Commission.

Collinson, Peter (1963), *The Cutteslowe Wall*, London, Faber & Faber.

Dunleavy, Patrick (1981), *Politics of Mass Housing in Britain*, Oxford, Clarendon Press.

Engels, Friedrich (1892), *The Condition of the Working Class in England in 1844*, London, Swan Sonnenschein & Co.

Fabian Society (2000), *Commission on Taxation and Citizenship*, London, Fabian.

Fletcher, Mike (2004), *The Making of Liverpool*, Barnsley, Wharncliffe Books.

Foley, Julie (2004), *The Problems of Success: Reconciling Economic Growth and the Quality of Life in the South East*, London, IPPR.

Foot, Michael (1973), *Aneurin Bevan*, London, Davis-Poynter.

Gaudie, Edith (1974), *Cruel Habitations*, London, Allen & Unwin.

Gifford, Lord, Brown, Wally and Bundey, Ruth (1989) *Loosen the Shackles*, London, Karia Press.

Greater London Authority (2000), *Homes for a World City*, London, GLA.

Greater London Authority (2000), *Towards A London Plan*, London, GLA.

Greater London Authority (2002), *Draft London Plan*, London, GLA.

Greater London Authority (2003), *Draft London Plan, Panel Report*, London, GLA.

Greater London Authority (2003), *London Household Survey*, London, GLA.

Greater London Authority (2005), *Housing Capacity Study*, London, GLA.

Hall, Sir Peter (1973), *The Containment of Urban England*, London, George Allen & Unwin.

Hennessy, Peter (1992), *Never Again*, London, Jonathan Cape.

Hill, Octavia (1883), *Homes of the London Poor*, London, Macmillan.

Hole, James (1985 [1866]), *The Home of the Working Class*, London, Garland.

Holmans, Alan (2005), 'The context for housing policy since 1975, Statistical Times series with commentary', London, ODPM.

Holmans, Alan, Monk, Sarah and Whitehead, Christine (2004), *Building for the Future*, London, Shelter.

Holmes, Chris (2005), *The Other Notting Hill*, Warwickshire, Brewins Forum on Social Housing.

Housing Green Paper (2000), *Quality and Choice*, London, HMSO.

Institute for Public Policy Research (2000), *Forum for Social Housing*, London, IPPR.

Labour Party (1945), *Let's Face the Future*, London, Labour Party.

London Housing Board (2005), *Capital Homes: The London Housing Strategy, 2005–2016*, London, Government Office for London.

London Housing Board Task Force, (2004), *Sustainable Communities: Mobility and Choice*, London, Government Office for London.

McDonald, Alan (1986), *The Weller Way*, London, Faber.

McLean, Iain (2004), 'Land tax: options for reform' in paper for IPPR/Oxford seminar on 'New Politics of Ownership'.

Macmillan, Harold (1969), *Tides of Fortune*, London, Macmillan.

Maxwell, Dominic (2004), *Fair Dues: Towards a More Progressive Inheritance Tax*, London, IPPR.

Mayhew, Henry (1851), *London Labour and the Working Poor*, London, Macmillan.

Mayor's Housing Commission (2000*)*, *Homes for a World City*, London, GLA.

Mearns, Andrew (1883), *The Bitter Cry of Outcast London*, London, Frank Cass.

Morgan, Kenneth (1984), *Labour in Power 1945–51*, Oxford, Clarendon Press.

Muellbauer, John (2004), *Property and Land, Taxation and the Economy after the Barker Review*, York, Joseph Rowntree Foundation.

Nevin, Brendan, Lee, Peter, Goodson, Lisa, Murie, Alan and Phillimore, Jenny (2001) *Changing Housing Markets and Urban Regeneration in the M62 Corridor*, Birmingham, Centre for Urban and Regional Studies.

North Islington Housing Rights Project (1974), *Street by Street*, London, Shelter.

Notting Hill Housing Service (1968), 'Report of Housing Survey' London, Notting Hill Housing Service.

Office of the Deputy Prime Minister (2005), *Sustainable Communities: Homes for All*, London, ODPM.

Page, David (1993), *Building for Communities: a Study of New Housing Association Estates*, York, Joseph Rowntree Foundation.

Page, David and Boughton, Rosie, (1998) *Housing Today*, London.

Patrick, R. and Jacobs, M. (2003), *Wealth's Fair Measure*, London Fabian Society.

Pawson, Hal and Fancy, Cathie (2003), *Maturing Assets*, Bristol, Policy Press.

Paxton, Will and Wynner, Ruth (2001), *The Asset Effect*, London, IPPR.

Power, Anne (1987), *Property before People*, London, Allen & Unwin.

Power, Anne (1997), *Estates on the Edge*, Basingstoke, Macmillan.

Prime Minister's Strategy Unit (2003), *London Analytical Report*, London, Cabinet Office.

Prime Minister's Strategy Unit (2004), *London Project Report*, London, Cabinet Office.

Ravetz, Alison (2000), *Council Housing and Culture*, London, Routledge.

Reiss, Richard (1918), *The Home I Want*, London, Hodder & Stoughton.

Rowbotham, Sheila (1973*), Hidden from History*, London, Pluto Press.

Rowntree, Seebohm (1901), *Poverty: a Study in Town Life*, London, Macmillan.

Rowntree, Seebohm (1917), Memorandum for Housing Panel in England and Wales of the Ministry of Reconstruction, London.

Royal Commission on the Distribution of the Industrial Population, (1940), Cmnd 6153, London, HMSO.

Samuel, R. (1962), *New Left Review*, London, Verso.

Sanderson, T. H. (ed.) (1894), *Speeches and Addresses of Edward Henry XVth Earl of Derby/E. Henry*. Vol 1, London, Longmans Green & Co.

Social Exclusion Unit (1998), *Strategy for Neighbourhood Renewal*, London, SEU.

Social Exclusion Unit (2000), *A New Commitment to Neighbourhood Renewal*, London, SEU.

Stedman Jones, Gareth (1971), *Outcast London*, Oxford, Clarendon Press.

Stephens, Mark, Burns, Nicky and Mackay, Lisa (2002), *Social Market or Safety Net*, London, Policy Press.

St Mungo's (2004) *Annual Report*, available online at www.mungos. org (accessed 02/11/05).

Terry, Rachel (2005), *HomeSave*, Coventry and London, Chartered Institute of Housing and Shelter.

Tindall, Gillian (1977), *The Fields Beneath*, London, Maurice Temple Smith.

Tudor Walters Committee on Standards of Local Authority Housing (1918), London, HMSO.

Unwin, Raymond (1912), *Nothing Gained by Overcrowding*, London, King & Son.

Waddilove, Lewis (1983), *New Earswick*, York, Joseph Rowntree Foundation.

Walterton and Elgin Community Homes (1998), *Against the Odds*, London, W&E Community Homes Ltd.

White, Jerry (2001), *London in the Twentieth Century*, London, Penguin.

Wilcox, Steve (2004), Taxation Issues, *UK Housing Review 2004/5*, York, Joseph Rowntree Foundation.

Wilkinson, Tony (1981), *Down and Out*, London, Quarter Books.

Young, Ken and Garside, Pat (1982*), Metropolitan London: Politics and Urban Change*, London, Edward Arnold.

Young, Ken and Kramer, John (1978), *Strategy and Conflict in Metropolitan Housing*, London, Heinemann.

Index

Pages containing relevant illustrations and tables are indicated by *italic* type.